BOOK OF MAN:

A NAVY SEAL'S GUIDE TO THE LOST ART OF MANHOOD

By Derrick F. Van Orden

with Adam Mitchell

This book is dedicated to my favorite person in the world, Sara Jane, and the four children she has given me.

And as of April, our first grandchild, Little Madelyn

Book of Man: A Navy SEAL's Guide
To The Lost Art Of Manhood
© 2015 by Derrick F. Van Orden

Cover design by SP Publishing, LLC
Interior design by Lindsey Khamphouy
Illustrations by Abby Van Orden

ISBN 978-0-692-42737-8

BOOK OF MAN:

A NAVY SEAL'S GUIDE TO THE LOST ART OF MANHOOD

By Derrick F. Van Orden

with Adam Mitchell

TABLE OF CONTENTS

AUTHOR'S NOTE

Many of the actions described in this book are inherently dangerous; as a matter of fact, many of them are incredibly dangerous, and several of them are simply stupid. By no means should they be attempted unless you are under the direct supervision of a trained professional. Even then, I would not recommend doing them unless you have made peace with your Maker. There have been many times when I have wondered how I have managed to still be on the right side of the dirt, so to speak. Additionally, the names used in this book are real if they are a featured writer, otherwise they have been changed, and, lastly, the events that are described herein are as accurate as my memory can make them.

Remember, though, I am a Sailor and these are my Sea Stories...

.

INTRODUCTION

T he idea to write this book occurred to me years ago when I when I began to notice that American men no longer appear to understand some of the most basic skills that used to be associated with manhood.

I know that every older generation says this about younger men, but I think this has become particularly pronounced due to the rapid increase of the integration of technology in our everyday lives. Although technology has always fascinated men in particular, it is getting to the point where young men now spend more time in virtual worlds than with real humans. It seems that unless it takes batteries or can be plugged in, there is little to no interest in actually *doing* something or speaking to someone face-to-face these days. With this isolation from each other there seems to be a rise in dehumanization of our society. We think of people as avatars, not flesh and blood.

Not all things old are bad; some things that have been forgotten need to be remembered. There are *so many* things that I think we have forgotten. Most of them are simple skills, but they have just vanished like my washboard abs and hair. Can you sharpen a knife? Can you build a fire? Can you bait a hook with a worm? Fifty years ago, these would all be silly questions, but today they are completely valid.

American men are becoming so far removed from the real, physical world that some of us do not even realize that these are important skills to have. Our fathers, grandfathers, and great-grandfathers would be astounded that we do not how to perform these simple tasks. In short, American men today can tweet pictures of their genitals around the world in an instant, but many have no idea how to change a tire. This is so prevalent in our society that people don't even understand the *concept* of manhood any longer. When I was discussing the idea of this book to a friend of mine—a man who is considered successful on many levels, including as a husband and in business—he said: "I know exactly what you mean, I tell guys 'If you don't have a real estate license, you better get on it, you are way behind.' I looked at him and said: "That is exactly the opposite of what I am talking about." A real estate license will not keep you warm and fed in the woods. Basic man skills will.

You may notice the tone of this book may seem harsh at times. This is intentional. The world perceives Americans as soft and spoiled, and, unfortunately, I find this to be true more often than not. This is not a political statement. On the contrary, it is a reflection; it is an observation. I think that we can and should be better than we are, and this is what I am choosing to do about it.

Why Me, Not You

You may be asking yourself why I am qualified to write a book like this in the first place. Of all the people in the world, why should I be the one trusted to put pen to paper, or fingers to keyboard, to define and articulate the requirements for an entire country's gender? A quick bio: My name is Derrick Van Orden, and I am a 26-year veteran of the United States Navy and SEAL Teams. I've served in every United States military Combatant Command (COCOM) as a SEAL, including in the European Command as a Joint Commissioned Observer (JCO) under the NATO Stabilization Force (SFOR) in the former Yugoslavia during the Bosnian War, U.S. Southern Command, U.S. Pacific Command, U.S. Africa Command, and with U.S. Central Command for multiple tours in both Afghanistan and Iraq.

I am also a founding member of the organization responsible for training West Coast SEALs for combat, where I was instrumental in the development of both the Land Warfare and Special Reconnaissance curricula which are now the foundation of the advanced training that SEALs receive prior to deployment. I have served as the Senior Enlisted Leader for a 120+ Task Unit deployed to multiple combat theaters simultaneously, the lead contingency operations planner for all Special Operations Forces in Europe, and the senior SEAL career specialist responsible for shaping the SEAL force to meet the challenges of a constantly changing world.

I never claimed to do any of these well, I am just saying I did them.

In addition to being a retired Navy SEAL Senior Chief, I am also a former paramedic and a man of faith. I have starred in a major motion picture and am an author and poet. I have traveled the world several times, mostly with a gun. I can tell a joke and cook an animal I harvested over a fire that I started. I hate thieves. I know how to sew and play cards, but I don't gamble. I open doors for all people, use good manners, and can arrange flowers. I have been knocked out fighting and have knocked other men out. I do not respect positional authority and encourage others not to. I am a fan of human rights and have risked my life defending them.

Of all the things I mentioned above, I am going to guess that the one you are most interested in is the Navy SEAL bit. I make this assumption because I can't remember that last time someone asked me how to cook a squirrel or make a centerpiece for the dinner table, but people ask me about being a SEAL almost every day. There is a natural curiosity surrounding my former profession and a ton of books that have been written by and about us lately. This may be a work worth mentioning or a fart in the wind; only time will tell.

Why do I mention my lengthy list of credentials? I can assure you it isn't to blow my own horn, so to speak, but to convey the fact that I have long-term experience in many different environments. I have a particularly unique world view. I gained this world view by living with people in their huts—cooking, hunting, and fighting with them. My experiences are practical, not theoretical.

My career path has given me the opportunity to work with people of incredibly high caliber, as well as train and mentor young men starting out with very limited knowledge and life skills. Fortunately, along the way I have also taken the time to stop and learn from others with more advanced knowledge than mine.

In my mind, this is at the very core of being a man. I understand and respect the fact that if you have paid taxes, you paid for my training. I also acknowledge that when I was away, many of you, particularly police officers and firefighters, were here protecting my family. I owe you a debt, and sharing my experiences with you is one small way I can repay you. Thank you for keeping us all safe on the home front. I will shake your hand every time I see you.

Why Them, Not Me

You'll learn as you continue to read this book that I don't view my former occupation, being a Navy SEAL, as the sole qualification for being a man. As a result, I have asked many others to contribute their knowledge and expertise to this book. Each of them, for some reason or another, had an influence on me developing into a man and provided me with a bit of strength, wisdom, guile, and courage. Some of them I've known my entire life and others I have only recently met. They include other former Navy SEALs, studio owners, stunt men, a book publisher, insurance agent, karate fighter, banker, haberdasher, graphic novelist, and an Academy-Award-winning actor. What they have in common is that I view them all as men, not merely as males. Each one has done something which I view as critical to manhood. They've seen a challenge, accepted the challenge, and persevered until they accomplished the goal. They are all servants.

Also, I just like talking about my friends. I wish this book were bigger so you could meet more of them.

These men are part of my Tribe. I feel sorry for the people that think a "tribe" is based on race, geographic region, or religion. Those who do this are lesser men.

There is a noted difference between being a male and being a man. Although a man and a male both have external genitalia, there's only one that can be counted on in a pinch. Being a man is just that. Being a male is nothing special. It's the guy that you hear complaining about everything but never lifting a finger to make a positive change. He is the smartest man on the Internet, who hides behind the anonymity of a screen to bully people. He is the guy that expects everything to be given to him simply because he exists. He abuses the power he has been given, either physical or positional, for personal gain or pleasure. A *man* on the other hand will go out of his way to solve a problem, earn his keep, take care of his family, and be respectful to the people around him at all times, even if he is about to kill them.

Although this book is titled *Book of Man, A Navy SEAL's Guide to the Lost Art of Manhood*, this book is written for more than that audience. It is a book for young boys who want to be a Man; Men who are young boys, who need to grow up and be a Man; and women and girls who want an actual Man. Granted, I don't think a thirteen-year-old boy or girl needs to know how to "pit" another vehicle in a car chase, or how to make a Manhattan, but these are included because this book is written to be intergenerational. It is also written to be read more than once and reflected on.

This is an analog book for the digital world. It might give you a glimpse at what my friend Mouse McCoy calls the "20th Century Man."

On a very important note, being raised by a single mother, I will not entertain a discussion of how this book can be construed as misogynistic. It simply is not. I love my mother dearly and respect her as a human being. She is, in fact, one of the better fathers a guy could have.

I encourage you, all of you, to read this book as it was intended: a slightly irreverent look at the world of mankind from my perspective. Hopefully it will fill some gaps in your life that you may not know exist.

Derrick F. Van Orden
Coronado, CA 2015

CHAPTER I

What It Means To Be A Man Vs. Being A Male

Before I joined the military, I didn't think much about what it meant to be a man. As a young boy, I didn't have many male figures to look up to other than Gunnery Sergeant Robert F. Mulligan, United States Marine Corps, now retired. Also known as my Uncle Bob. I was drawn to the way he carried himself because he had been in the military, was currently the police chief and fire chief of a small Wisconsin town, and was confident, calm, and strong. He was raised on a farm in rural Minnesota and joined the Navy at sixteen years old to go to World War II, and I think that says a lot about him. He was bored, tired of farm life and the hectic nature of his ever-expanding family that would peak at ten with him and his brothers and sisters. He wanted an adventure. He was the oldest and was helping support his brothers and sisters by selling milk and whatever else they could produce on the farm. Uncle Bob was always aware of and in charge of his environment, and, maybe most importantly, he was a servant and protector of his fellow man. In my life there have not been that many people that I have known directly who have influenced me in the way I look at the world, but Uncle Bob was certainly one of the early ones.

My First Gunfight

I was drawn to the military life for a reason I simply can't articulate, but I remember very clearly participating in my first BB gun war when I was about ten years old.

After my mother had purchased a green plastic USMC helmet for me, I was sure I was invincible. My friend had positioned himself on the edge of a recently plowed cornfield behind our house, and I was slowly sneaking up to snipe him, weaving my way through the furrows to get close enough. Just as I got into range, he noticed me and pivoted to shoot. I ducked down, leaving just my shiny new helmet exposed over the small mound of dirt, sure in my defensive position and armored protection. Then, POP! I instantly had a searing pain in the middle of my forehead. I ran my hand between my eyes and felt a growing lump where a BB had smacked into my flesh. My helmet had failed me. I learned a valuable lesson that day, and it is one that I immediately forgot and seem to remember and forget regularly: Like so many things in life, we think we know what we are doing at the start, but then very rapidly learn that we do not have any idea as time moves on.

This is exactly what happened when I joined the Navy.

I went into the Navy on a whim and to get out of Dodge. I was screwing up by the numbers as a young man. I dropped out of school at sixteen just like my uncle and was a nearly complete slip turd for two years until I finally realized I needed a change. After enlisting, I explained my "enhanced experimentation techniques" with marijuana to the recruiter and wound up working on a tugboat. Apparently the only job the Navy trusted me to do was work on a boat pulling ships loaded with hundreds of thousands of pounds of bombs and ammunition in and out of port. I still do not get this.

I soon decided there must be something better than painting boats and cleaning toilets in the Navy, so I started to pay attention to what was taking place around me. Unlike today, there were not a ton of movies and books about SEALs, and I did not even know what the term meant.

SEAL is an acronym that stands for: SEa, Air, and Land. These are the three mediums we use to get to and from an operation. Interestingly enough, these are also the three mediums everyone else uses to get to and from the office. The real difference is what you plan on doing when you get to the office.

Most people surf the Internet, talk about television shows by the water cooler, and try to leave work by five o'clock every day. SEALs do these things, but with guns and knives, and often underwater.

As a Navy veteran, and in between chasing skirts and eating fish chowder, President Kennedy decided to create what would become the Navy SEALs. This was slid under the radar, so to speak, during his famous May 25, 1961 speech about sending someone to the moon. The first SEAL Teams were commissioned in 1962, and in 1983 the remaining Underwater Demolition Teams (UDT) were converted to SEAL Teams. Navy SEALs come from a proud heritage. Starting with the Scouts and Raiders in WWII, through the Naval Combat Demolition Units (NCDUs), and finally the Underwater Demolition Teams, (UDTs), there have been Frogmen fighting for this country for a very long time.

Basic Underwater Demolition/SEAL (BUD/S) training is where all Sailors, officer and enlisted, are forged into SEALs. It is arguably the hardest military training in the world. I personally don't care to have this argument; there are so many more things to argue about like should curling be an Olympic sport. I just know that on the scale of easy to you-have-got-to-be-shitting-me, it fell into the latter category. Even amongst my friends and colleagues in the Special Operations Forces (SOF) community, we talk about this, but the guys that get really worked up about it never had to rely on their fellow SOF operators when it really mattered. I think that we can all agree that SEAL training is very difficult. If this were not true, you would be reading "The Gas-Pumper's Practical Guide To..."

On the curling thing, I had the chance to do it once, and it is a hoot. About a half an hour into the game, the guy who was showing us how to play just stopped and said, "Let's get a beer." I asked if this was a regular break time in the game and he replied, "No, you just get a beer when you want to." Now you tell me curling should not be an Olympic sport.

An Accidental SEAL

I had a friend named Pat who was a corpsman, a Navy medic. He was always so chipper and seemed to really enjoy working at the base clinic. Additionally, Pat worked with corps-women, and his hands were never covered in paint as mine were. I don't think he even knew what a toilet brush was. I started working at the base clinic during my off hours, and after several months of studying, doing correspondence courses, and completing on the job training, I was given a slot to Hospital Corpsman School (Corps School) in San Diego, California.

 One day during class, we were told that the SEAL motivator was coming to speak to us. By that time, I had met three fellow students who had joined the Navy to be SEALs. When I asked them what this was, they told me you get to run around, shoot guns, and blow things up. And that it was ludicrously difficult to make it through training. When I immediately said, "I'll do that," they all laughed at me. Then, the motivator came into the class and said, "I am Chief Randy, if you want to be a SEAL come talk to me, if you do not, F you. You will probably quit anyway." And with that, Chief Randy turned and walked out of the classroom.

That was the best motivational speech I had ever heard. Chief Randy was the first of many examples I would eventually meet in the military of what I would later come to know as being a man. Strong willed, self-confident, sharp as a tack, and a no-nonsense professional. I was sold and had finally found my calling.

I did not have an easy time getting to BUD/S as I was not a proficient swimmer, and I did not see the need to quit smoking as I was a nimble guy who had years of experience running from the police so endurance was not an issue. The poor swimming was due to lack of knowing how to do the sidestroke, not being winded. As a future "Combatant Swimmer," the actual job title of a SEAL when I was going to school, this was not ideal. The system is radically different now: There are folks that mentor and coach guys along until they get into the Navy. Once they do, they are separated from the regular Navy guys in boot camp and spend more time exercising and getting prepared for BUD/S training. Despite all of this, upwards of 80 percent of them still end up quitting. I worked hard and finally passed the test to get a shot at being a SEAL.

As would happen frequently in my life, my orders were screwed up, and I was stationed at Balboa Hospital until they got it straightened out. Due to my elite status as someone who was selected to attend SEAL training, I was assigned to the "Pretorian Guard" of the hospital—the guys who walked around with carts picking up dirty linen. Yes, I essentially collected soiled sheets for three months, and this drudgery was offset by mopping, so I could not complain.

During this time, I decided that if I was going to be a SEAL, I was probably going to be in the business of making dead people, so I thought it would be advantageous to get familiar with them. Every Wednesday morning, autopsies were conducted at the morgue in the basement of the hospital, and I volunteered to assist in them. This turned out to be both fascinating and disturbing at the same time, just like a good movie.

After three months, I set aside my nasty scrubs and headed off to become a SEAL. As I was about to walk through the back gate of the compound, I flicked out my last cigarette. I had learned that this habit would not be compatible with the exercise and whatnot. As I got closer to the "grinder," a large cement area where exercise is done, I started to hear yelling. Once I rounded the corner, I saw pandemonium: guys in various stage of dress getting hosed off, running around, doing PT, running out to the ocean and back, covered in sand, shouting.

I almost dropped my orders on the pavement and all I could think was, "What the hell did I get myself into?"

BUD/S turned out to be an incredible experience. I learned there that the human mind and body are fearfully and wonderfully made. We are capable of doing things that, when left to our own devises, we would never attempt because we thought them to be impossible. I saw strong men break and weak men take charge. I did not break.

My First SEAL Team

After graduating BUD/S I asked for and was assigned to SEAL Team FOUR in Virginia Beach, Virginia. At that time, each SEAL Team was assigned a geographic Area of Operations (AO). Team FOUR's AO was South and Central

America. I did not pick this team because I spoke Spanish or because I particularly wanted to go there; I picked it because it was the last SEAL Team to be involved in combat that I was aware of.

Just like I thought checking out dead people in the morgue would be helpful in being a SEAL, now that I was really on my way to being one, I thought I should go to combat. I strove every day to be the best, most qualified SEAL I could be to reach that goal. There are two questions you should ask yourself every day as a SEAL: "What have you learned to make yourself a better SEAL today?" And, "What have you done for America today?" These can and should be related. If you can't answer these questions, you need to go back to your cage where your gear is stored and figure something out. This is actually a universal man-truth as are so many listed in this book. If you care enough about something, you should consistently strive to become better at it, or make it better independent of you and your feelings. If more people humbly did this, I think our country and the world in general would be a much better place.

How to Become a SEAL

A bit of an explanation as to what the pipeline was and is for being a SEAL: In my era, a Sailor had to have some type of job in the Navy prior to going to BUD/S. This was called a "source rating." Mine, as you know now, was corpsman. Once you had a rating, you went to BUD/S for six months of training, although most people lasted only a month or so. Following this, you attended STT or SEAL Tactical Training, which is now called SEAL Qualification Training (SQT). This was an additional four months of advanced SEAL things. Graduating from this, you were assigned to a SEAL Team where you had to work for a minimum of six months in a platoon. Following this time, and with the recommendation of your Chief and Officer in Charge, you had the privilege to go to a "Trident Board" where you were tested on everything a SEAL needs to know by the people at the Team that knew it.

This can be a stressful event. If you passed your board, you were awarded the Naval Enlisted Code 5326 and your Naval Special Warfare insignia, the mighty Trident., also known as the "Budweiser" or, to us, the "Bird." Today, this happens after guys graduate from SQT. Not as exciting or rather suspenseful as when I attended, but you do get the ball rolling sooner.

To answer the question you just asked yourself in your head: No, I do not think training has gotten any easier. I think it has gotten a lot smarter. We did some things that I would not recommend, but I do believe *we* were harder because of it.

Notice please that I said harder, not necessarily smarter.

Once I had my Bird, I continued in my profession for an additional twenty-two years, eventually deploying as a SEAL to every Combatant Command and every continent except for Antarctica and Australia. (I did spend eight weeks or so training in New Zealand, but if I called this Australia, the Kiwis would put a hit out on me.)

Military Man

Some people think that you need to be or have been in the military in order to know how to properly be a man. To me, this is silly. Although it would seem important to be involved in a martial vocation, you eventually realize that it is more about who you are than what you do or where you have been. What is at the core of your identity as an individual? It is not if you wear a uniform or not. The uniform can be changed readily, whereas character takes time. I tell people that I have enough character to be in a Dickens novel. I have just never told them what character.

Along my path as I have encountered other young men from all walks of life, I have often thought about what it means to be a man. A friend of mine said that his father's definition of being a man is "a person that moves Earth," and if you think about it, there is a great deal of truth in that statement. Men interact positively with their environment and do things with their hands. They make and master machines. They accept responsibility and do what they say they're going to do. A man will back you up in a fight while others will just watch it happen. A male will think of a reason not to interact, shy away, and leave. Or better yet, record video of it with a smart phone and post it on the Internet. That's not saying all things man are based on or around violence, because they are not. They are actually based on *commitment*. If you're committed enough to somebody to actually get involved in fisticuffs, then you're a true friend. When you are willing to put yourself at risk for another human being, that is a reflection of manhood.

Just as men move earth with their hands, they have to be willing to risk harm in order to help others. This can be financial risk, social risk, or emotional risk. The point is, you either have skin in the game or not.

Men also identify problems and don't simply sit around waiting for someone else to come in and fix them. As my wife, Sara, and I have raised our four children, two being sons, we've often taken the time to explain that if they see a problem they need to take an interest in personally addressing it. One of the greatest philosophers of the twentieth century, Vanilla Ice, really encapsulated this message in his song "Ice Ice Baby" when he rapped, "If there was a problem, yo I'll solve it."

So what does it mean to be a man? And I would also ask, when did being a man become a punch line? In our society it's almost as if it is bad to say that you're a man, like it is wrong. A "manly man" is considered a joke as if you are not as civilized as the rest of the world.

When you go back to the dawn of time and evaluate legendary leaders, they tend to be strong men who are able to convey a clear vision of their intentions. In general, I believe people are attracted to following someone who is tough, resilient, and resolute. When you talk about the bond between leader and follower, friends and colleagues, this has not changed, and the dynamic will probably never vary because it is part of who we are; it is in our DNA.

Men are focused, motivated, and always seem to be going somewhere. They are driven and kinetic. "Kinetic" is a term often overused by the military in reference to things such as "kinetic operations," which generally refer to bombs, explosions, and casualties. But this is very different. It means movement, action in the physics term of kinetic energy, not just potential. They're not just wandering around aimlessly. They're starting at point A and continuing to a defined point B.

So, what drives people into action? Many attach their goals to what they think is important such as money, fame and material goods, but this has nothing to do with the actual makeup of the man or the human being for that matter. You *have* money; you *are not* money. This whole material society is horse shit. There is no polite way to say it.

Personally, what has motivated me is not the desire for success and the things that accompany it, but the fear of failure. What people don't understand any longer is the importance of failure.

In our society today, we don't expect others to hold us accountable for our actions and failures; we just don't want to be bothered. We don't even want to hold ourselves accountable. This has got to change. We must hold others and ourselves accountable for each other's actions. If we collectively lived that way as a society I would venture to say that we would have many more successes.

As time moves on and everything is continually becoming safeguarded, failure is missing more and more from our everyday experiences. Everyone getting a trophy and not keeping score at games is destroying our country and lives as it removes incentive and the basic knowledge of where we stand. It is simply junk. Life outside the protective bubble of America is not like that. If you are not the fastest runner in the Olympics, you lose; if you are not the strongest and smartest in a fight, you can die. That is how the world works, and we are screwing the next generation by pretending otherwise. In BUD/S this is hammered home every day. "It pays to be a winner," means something there.

Training to the point of failure is critical if we are going to improve. Living your life without failure is impossible, but if you train hard enough, failing when it counts will become less and less frequent in your life. It's not the goal or desired end state but it's a tool that can be used by people in order to better themselves. Being afraid of letting others down is an incredibly powerful force, and being afraid to fail, not because you're going to be embarrassed but because you're going to let folks down, can drive you to curl up into a ball in the corner out of paralyzing fear or can drive you to excel.

Men choose the latter, and it is a choice.

Admitting your failure should not be something that is avoided because it is viewed in our society as being weak. Personally, I believe that when you're capable of admitting your failures you're the strongest person in the room.

What Really Matters in Life

I realized when I was a young man that I was not going to be capable of collecting objects because my family was so poor that the only option I had was to collect connections instead. As I've grown, I've tried to show my children the importance of connections between human beings and developing a network of friends. Our connectedness is what makes us strong. And I don't mean in some kooky spiritual way or "we're all part of one big spaghetti bowl" kind of deal. I actually have no idea what that means; it just sounded appropriate. I think if we understood the connections between us as a race and not individual *races* we'd be better off. "Mankind" should mean something, precisely because it is so imprecise a term.

So, what is a true friend, and how do we help one another? There are all these little funny sayings like, "I got your back, bro," that appear to be very popular. What does that even mean? Is your back going to do something that needs to be stopped? Let us suppose that you *don't* have my back. Let us suppose you say that you have my back and you don't. What happens? In the regular world, nothing. I mean you could be a little angry with somebody, but that's it. In my former vocation as a Navy SEAL, there could definitely be some negative consequences by telling someone that you had their back and you didn't. The first one is, if they didn't die they were probably going to kick your ass later for lying or being a turd. I would call this a form of accountability, and I don't know when that became a bad concept, we talked about this.

Having someone's back means that you will protect them as they move forward to accomplish a common goal. In a way it is self-serving because you are, by default, following someone who is taking you where you want to go.

Sure, men can stand alone, but not for long. The man versus nature solo deal? It just doesn't work in the long run. Eventually, you need companionship, friendship, and brotherhood. That's just how we're made. We will become the tripped-out rhesus monkey with the carpet mom if we are not in the company of other humans for too long of a time. If you don't know what I am talking about, look it up, it is disturbing.

So what happened? Once people started working essentially as cogs in a machine, they became separate from each other even though they were standing right next to one another. The greater our ability to "communicate" through new technology becomes, it seems the less we are able to actually understand each other. There appears to be an inverse relationship with the amount of technology involved and the actual connection between human beings, even though the technology is built to facilitate that.

If you are going to make an impression on the Earth and the rest of the world, you have to be able to influence people to do what is right and good. For myself, I think the first steps towards becoming a man are when you really start to see yourself as a separate person and understand that there are different requirements on you and that you're responsible for things. In other words, you need to seek out problems, learn how to solve those problems, and do it. The best way to do this is by understanding how things work.

Welcome.

CHAPTER II

Weapons

Weapons have been around for a very long time, as long as there have been rocks and people. Mostly lazy or mean people. I say "lazy" because someone can toil the soil for months, or go out hunting to gather food, and just as they sit down to enjoy a salad or steak, another person can walk up behind them and hit them over the head with a rock. Mean people will do that even if food is not at stake.

My First Gun

Growing up, I did not have many guns around because my mother was not a real fan of them. My father was a fan of making children rather than raising them, so, as a young boy, I did not have much adult supervision when it came to the *Way of the Gun*. My first real weapon was a Crosman 760 Pumpmaster™ .177 caliber pellet/BB gun. I don't remember where it came from, or who gave it to me, but it was a prized possession. You may scoff at this, but when I had that war machine in my hands, I was unstoppable. Like many youngsters, I didn't have a lot of responsibilities, especially during the summer when my biggest concern was whether I would be able to scrape enough money together to buy BBs. When I could afford ammunition, I would take my gun and go into the woods in southern Wisconsin. If you were a small creature within twenty-five yards of my gun and me, trust me, you were going to get a little sugar. Of course, I encourage much more responsible use of weapons now that I'm a little older, but at that age I killed anything that moved. If I didn't have money for BBs I would find an anthill to blast away at. This way I could recover the BBs from the anthill, dust them off, put them back in my gun, and shoot them again. I will say that there were many small creatures, from ants to a mud hen, which fell to the mighty boom stick that was my Crosman.

Your perception changes when you have a gun. Even as a small child you are capable of wielding formerly unheard of power, and this feeling can be intoxicating. I don't think this is necessarily a good or a bad thing, but I do think the respect this power demands is often taken too lightly. It is something that can and should be taught, preferably from a young age.

Passing on the Legend

When my wife, Sara, was pregnant with our third child, Teddy, I was stationed at Virginia Beach, Virginia, and immediately after we went to the hospital to get the first or second sonogram, the one where they tell you if it's a boy or a girl, I dropped Sara off at home and drove directly to Walmart. What did I buy? You guessed it: a Crosman 760, the very same BB/pellet gun I grew up with.

Yes, my son, in fact, was armed *in utero*. No better time than the present, or I guess the future, to start training.

Although you aren't allowed to do this any longer, I took that BB gun on a deployment to South and Central America. We spent the first five weeks of living in the jungle at place called Camp McFaul, which is named after Chief Petty Officer Donald McFaul who was killed in the Panama invasion. With that gun, I shot a *fer-de-lance* snake, a deadly pit viper, and various jungle animals, including a bunch of termites.

Why did I take it with me into the jungle to shoot things? So it would be bloodied.

"Bloodied" is an old term. I'm sure I could find out where it comes from, but I don't really care to, and, on top of that, if I look it up it might mean something completely different than what I think it does. Sometimes being a man means making up your own words and meanings. Actually, that is more of a SEAL thing. These terms are normally used together, not always. To me, it means to be tested when it counts, particularly in the martial fields. I wanted this weapon to be tested and ready for when I would give it to my son. I can see how this may be perceived as weird in our culture now. In other cultures, this ritual is perfectly acceptable.

Guns - Good or Bad

Let's get something out of the way here regarding weapons, just to put it to bed. People often forget that a gun is simply a tool that can be used to create both negative and positive outcomes such as hunting for food or fighting to ensure that half of the planet does not speak solely German and the other half Japanese. A gun left to its own devices will do neither harm nor good. It is an object, an object with great potential, just like a plane or a car. You might say: "But guns are designed to cause harm." And I would say not necessarily, and, even if they were, that fact would be irrelevant because they can clearly be used for altruistic means. And, yes, I mean altruistic. Using weapons to stop someone from doing harm to others has an effect on the one who pulls the trigger. To say that planes and cars are okay because they were designed for a neutral purpose is to deny their potential use for destruction, hence September 11, 2001 and every time a drunk driver kills someone. The difference is intent. Enough of that, you get the point.

Another disclaimer. I spent an hour or so on the phone today with some lawyers. They are nice guys guys, but I want that time back on my deathbed. They are very concerned that you, the reader, will run out and buy a gun and shoot yourself or someone else because you read this book. I tried to explain to them that one of the main themes of this book was taking responsibility for your own actions, and that by over-cautioning you, I am not allowing you to take responsibility. Well, here we are. Guns are loud. Guns also shoot bullets that go for a very long way, even if you do not want them to. They also "kick" and could hurt your shoulder. Guns are sometimes made of wood, and you could get a splinter if the stock is cracked or chipped. Guns are also made of metal, and if you were to keep one in the freezer and then touch your tongue to it, it would stick and be uncomfortable and embarrassing. They are heavy, so if you drop it on your foot, you might hurt it. Your foot that is. Guns can also be shiny so you should wear sunglasses. I think that is about it. If you really want to get involved with firearms, go to your local gun store of range and get into a weapon/hunter's safety course.

What Are These Things of Wonder?

It seems some people either know a lot about guns these days or nothing at all. Just like farming. For starters, guns come in different calibers, which basically indicates the size of the bullet. Caliber is the approximate internal diameter of the barrel of the gun and the diameter of the projectile it fires. These need to be very close or exactly the same, or you are going to have significant issues. This measurement is usually shown in millimeters or in hundredths or thousandths of an inch. As you can imagine, the larger the caliber of the rifle, the bigger the kick it will provide when fired.

There are pistols—the short ones—and then rifles, which are generally longer than pistols. You stick these up against your shoulder when you shoot them, unless you are in a movie or are a jackass, or are a jackass in a movie. A shotgun is a type of rifle, but most are not "rifled." The term "rifling" describes the grooves that are carved inside of the barrel in a twisting pattern. This makes a bullet spin as it travels through the air, which gives it stability and allows it to stay straighter for a longer period of time.

The first to really master the spinning of a bullet was a Frenchman named Claude-Étienne Minié, who created the first muzzle-loading, spin-stabilized bullet called the "Minié ball" in the mid-1800s, which wasn't really shaped like a ball at all. It was a conical-cylindrical soft lead bullet used during the Crimean War and American Civil War, which killed an amazing amount of soldiers because of its accuracy.

Friends and Mentors.

I have included input from a former colleague who wishes to remain anonymous. By former colleague I mean at one point I trained him and at another I worked for him. He wishes to remain anonymous because he is still on active duty and does not want to have his personal comments construed as speaking for the community as some of our SEALs have been want to do in the recent past. As a retired Frogman I have the pleasure of speaking only for me, while in uniform, he does not. It may seem ironic to many people that those who protect our Constitutional Rights and ensure our freedom actually give up some of their own rights while in service to their country-but like me they do it willingly because that is what Men and Women do. They subordinate their needs for the needs of others. To be sure his comments were reviewed by the DOD, as has this entire book, to ensure that nothing in here jeopardizes national security or our brother's and sister's still in harm's way. My friend is now a Commanding Officer (CO). In the SEAL Teams, we use the term "Skipper" for the CO. Regular Navy guys sometimes view that term negatively, but we don't. The thing about the Navy Skipper in general and this Skipper in particular, Sailors take this position very seriously. There are times when this respect is not warranted. My good friend has earned his position by performing exceptionally in combat and in peacetime. The respect I accord to him and Officers of his ilk is unwavering. He is an example of what SEALs think of when we think of a Leader of men. He is additionally a devoted husband and father. Two more reasons to have him in this book.

Weapon Safety

CDR X

Commanding Officer SEAL Team

When VanO (that's what we call him) asked me to contribute to his book by providing some fundamental firearm safety rules I was not very surprised since much of our interaction over the course of the last dozen years involved me cautioning safety to him. Many of our adventures together began with VanO saying, "Hey, I was thinking let's try this..." and off the reservation we'd go. But, we'll save those Sea Stories for VanO's second book which I have recommended he titles "The Book of Man I am screwed, a collection of short stories" In all seriousness, I am honored to contribute to this great book and honored to be friends with a man who is so diabolically clever yet so wholeheartedly good. He is an incredible SEAL, mentor, husband, Father, Teammate and most of all a great teller of tales, most of which are true.

Five basic rules of firearms safety.

Firearms are tools and like all tools there are proper and improper ways to use them. There are rules and techniques for their use and with time and practice anyone can master these tools and techniques. I learned from the beginning to treat these particular tools with respect and in such a way that safety is emphasized. While mission accomplishment is paramount in the Teams, managing risk and increasing the safety of our force underpins every action we take. We do dangerous things as safely as possible. There are many more rules in my community for other tasks and tools, some complex and some simpler but adhering to these simple rules while shooting will keep you and your friends alive and ensure only the things you want to destroy with your weapon get destroyed. Additionally, adherence to these rules serves as an example of your professionalism and respect for firearms. No matter where you go if you follow these rules on a range and around other shooters, you will be recognized as a man who understands responsible firearm usage.

Five basic rules of firearms:

1. Treat every firearm as if it is loaded.

2. Never point a firearm at anything you are not willing to destroy.

3. Never put your finger on the trigger until you are ready to fire the weapon.

4. Always identify your target and what is beyond it.

5. Take your weapon off 'Safe' just before shooting, return it to 'Safe' when you are done shooting.

Sighting in the Weapon

When you have a gun that's not sighted in, essentially what you have is a noisemaker. Seriously. That's really about it. Sure, there is a chance that you might hit what you're aiming at, but it is a very small chance. There's a saying that we have in the SEAL Teams: "We don't want a scared enemy, we want a dead enemy." In order to accomplish this, your weapon has to be sighted in so you can hit your target. This process entails properly lining up the rear sight, the front sight, the barrel, and your eye for a certain distance. When you get these things in line and pull the trigger, the bullet will go where you think it's going to go.

In the 1990s, I was working with an allied nation, trying to teach them various skills such as shooting techniques and patrolling tactics. The first thing we do is always make sure everybody's weapons are sighted in. One particular guy was shooting an FN FAL, pronounced "FN F-A-L." It shoots the 7.62 NATO round. The gun was originally designed and built in Belgium, but Brazil also manufactures it. When I asked this guy to shoot his weapon on the range, I noticed he put his hand on the bottom of the magazine instead of up on the fore-grip, the front part of the rifle, to steady himself. I thought it was kind of funny when he started shooting.

"No, let's get in a different position," I told him, taking his rifle in order to demonstrate exactly how he should be holding it. I tightly gripped the fore-grip of the weapon and firmly secured it into my shoulder. Then, I looked down the sights, lined it up, and shot three rounds. The fore-grip on an FN FAL gets incredibly hot when you start shooting rounds through it, so I immediately took my hand off the rifle.

I looked at the guy, and he started smiling. He was trying to be polite, when, in fact, he should have just called me a dumbass. What's the lesson there? How about listening to the guy who shoots a particular type of gun every day and understand why he's doing what he is doing.

Once I figured out that this guy actually knew how to operate the weapon safely, we started getting him "dialed in." This meant gradually going from a bunch of holes in the target with no pattern, to a bunch of shots with a much closer grouping. So, after he shot a few rounds, I adjusted the sights. Then he shot a few more, and I repeated the process. I eventually noticed that, although the group of bullet holes this guy was producing were getting progressively closer together, they started moving around the target in a weird fashion. You can usually spot when guys are making mistakes while firing their weapons. Either they are breathing wrong, or squeezing the trigger too hard, or they're jerking the trigger, or trying to shoot too quickly…but this fit into none of these patterns.

We kept shooting for about twenty minutes, and I started to get very frustrated. At one point, I took a step back and looked at his weapon again. That is when I realized that his front sight post was bent. Every time we were adjusting his sights, the warped front sight post was moving around at a different angle. I took my pair of pliers, straightened out his sight post, and from that point on the guy was "keyhole-ing," meaning he was shooting all his bullets in a small group, like the size of a keyhole into the bull's-eye.

Let's talk about the sights themselves. There are a bunch of different kinds. There are iron sights, which are the old metal type that you may be familiar with already. Then there are telescopic sights, which are scopes, and there are laser sights that are pretty easy to figure out because they are a laser beam. There's also a little thing on a shotgun that looks like a BB at the end of your barrel.

First of all, you need to figure out what type of sight you have. We're going to start with iron sights because they're the easiest, don't take batteries, and hardly ever break, unless they're bent like the one I just told you about on the guy's FN FAL and actually, those did not break, just bent. Because there are so many different kinds of sights, it's very difficult to explain all of them in totality.

 With iron sights there are both fixed and adjustable sights. An example of a fixed sight would be on an older pistol where there's just the front sight post, sticking up on the front, and a groove that is carved into the back of the pistol. You line up the top of the front sight with the top of the groove. This is the kind of sight on the old six shooters.

As soon as they're in proper alignment, you pull the trigger, and the bullet should go where you have aimed. Again, that's the goal of any type of sight.

If you're able to adjust sights, they're called adjustable sights, not too difficult there. That means the front post and the rear sights are movable, or either the front or the rear is movable. Generally speaking, elevation, meaning up or down, is done by the front sight post, like on an AR-15. You may know it as an M16 or an M4 rifle. The elevation will go up and down by the front sight post, but on this type of gun you can adjust it in the back by moving that sight up and down itself, too. It is a rather complicated iron sight, come to think of it.

Because there are so many types of iron sights—adjustable, fixed, and all that crap—I'm going to teach you the super basic way to do anything with sights.

Step One: Go to a range, have a known distance, and only shoot from that distance until you get your stuff down. We sight our rifles in for a three-hundred-yard battle sight zero. Oddly enough, one thousand inches, the ballistics for shooting a 5.56 round, which is your M16 round, are nearly the same for three hundred yards. Because of this, you could do a very accurate sight-in at one thousand inches, which is just about twenty-five yards.

Step Two: You want to shoot a group of bullets, at least three, before you make an adjustment. If those three bullets aren't in close proximity to each other, you're just a bad shot, and you need to practice on the basic fundamentals of shooting. Don't worry about your sights until you have a nice group; then you can start worrying about adjusting the sights. What you are trying to do is move the impact of the bullet towards the center, or the bull's-eye, of the target. Author's Note: Do not "chase the bullet," meaning move the way you are aiming at the target to compensate for not hitting the bull's-eye. If you do this, your weapon will never get sighted in properly.

The best way to remember how to do this, ups and downs and lefts and rights of the sight adjustment, is to take your dominant hand and you make a "V" like a peace symbol, or in reality, it started off as a victory symbol, so we are going to call it a victory symbol. Stick your index finger and your middle finger up, forming a V, and hold it exactly nine inches in front of your eyes. If it is not exactly nine inches this will not work. I am totally joking; it can really be any distance from your eye. Then take your other hand, and stick your index finger straight up in the air. Line those up together so that the tips of your fingers are in alignment. You will now need to pretend that your fingers have to stay in alignment, like they were both attached to the barrel of a gun, for instance. If you could not figure that out by yourself, I am seriously wondering if you should own a gun in the first place.

Then, focus on an object in the distance that will be the target you are aiming at. You should have two fingers back, one finger forward, on separate hands, and in the distance, an object. For instance, right now I'm driving my car and I'm doing this, and it's ludicrously dangerous and stupid, but I'm still going to do it, and I'm focusing on the Subaru symbol on the steering wheel. If I move the pointer finger of my left hand down—the one that's just by itself—and I want to align my fingers again on that object, I have to move everything up. This means if that were attached to a weapon, I would have to point the barrel farther up in the air to make the impact of the bullet go up. If I move the back—the two fingers in the victory symbol—and I move them to the right in order to align myself back up with my target, I have to shift everything in unison to the right This means the impact of the round will move to the right. The exact opposite is true if I move it to the left. You can practice this anywhere, but you should probably not do it in front of a post office or at the airport.

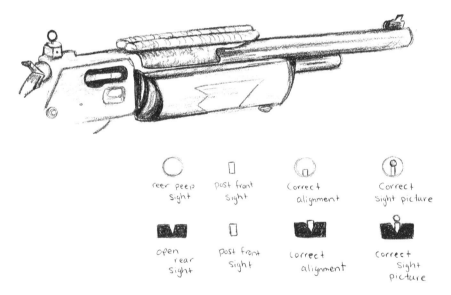

In a nutshell, that is how you sight in a weapon. Figure out if the front sight moves, the rear sight moves, or both of them move. Make sure you shoot a few rounds at a target from a known distance and continue until you get a good group. Then, adjust them appropriately by using your fingers. That's it, no more magic.

Scopes operate on the same principle, but they have cross hairs that you look at through a little glass window. The advantage of this little glass window is that is also magnifies what you are looking at. Just for clarity's sake, it does not actually make the object you are looking at bigger; it just makes it *look* bigger. Just like even though it seems like people on TV are talking to you, they are not. If you think they are, you absolutely do not need to own a gun. You should, however, immediately go to the kitchen and make a hat out of aluminum foil.

Just like iron sights, a scope has windage (left or right), and elevation (up or down) adjustments. They are generally round dials under small caps that are adjusted with a screwdriver or other such instrument. Every click means a different distance the bullet will move, so you are going to have to read the book on this.

I owe Larry a particularly large debt in that, prior to my retirement, he got in touch with me and asked if I would come out and work for him at Sealed Mindset Leaders. Having spent more time in the Navy than I have not, meaning I have been in the military longer than a civilian, this was greatly comforting to know I would have a relatively soft "landing pad" by working for a fellow SEAL and doing something meaningful. This was and is a big deal for my family and me. This is an example of what the SEAL Teams actually mean. Larry and his wife Anne were recently joined by Colt, the next up and coming Frogman.

Larry Yatch is a former SEAL and current CEO and founder of the Sealed Mindset family of companies: SEALed Mindset, SEALed Mindset Leaders and SEALed Mindset Matters. Sealed Mindset is a Navy SEAL-inspired defense training center (sealedmindset.com) that offers a variety of tools, training, and inspiration to grow confidence and overcome personal challenges. Sealed Mindset Leaders (smleaders.com) helps organizations develop proven leadership strategies and contingency-planning tools to remain competitive in a dynamic marketplace. Mindset Matters (mymindsetmatters.org) is a curriculum solution company that designs leadership and personal safety content for middle School and high School students to combat bullying and to build GRIT into our next generation of successful leaders.

Basic Shooting

By Larry Yatch

Her name was *Victoria*. She was sleek, elegant and powerful…and sometimes difficult to manage, especially when my adrenalin was high. When I spent time with her, I was quiet, focused, and relaxed—some say I was my best self. She was the perfect companion: understanding, but unyielding when I faltered. I couldn't imagine my life without her.

I first met her on a firing range when I politely told a sixty-five-year-old man (I was seven), that he wasn't following the range safety rules. I believe she inspired me then, she inspired me when I joined the Navy SEALs, and she continues to inspire me now as I educate others.

People assume that, as a Navy SEAL teaching defensive firearms, I'm teaching something elite or special I learned during my time in the Teams. Actually, as a five year old, I learned the fundamental knowledge needed to be safe around firearms from my Marine Corps veteran father. Those are the same lessons that served me through my time as a competitive shooter at the United States Naval Academy and through my time in combat as a Navy SEAL.

Since the beginning of man's time on this earth there has been a need for man to protect himself and those he cares for. Men have discovered and created tools to meet this most basic human need. Weapons began as tools that helped a man overcome his limitations, be it Jim Bowie's knife during the great sandbar duel, General Patton's ivory-gripped Colt 1911 pistol during the Battle of the Bulge, or Navy SEAL Chris Kyle's McMillan sniper rifle during the battle of Ramadi.

Even if you don't have any guns or think you will ever want a gun, *you will at some point in your life be exposed to a firearm*. If you do not know how to be safe around it, or how to use it correctly to protect yourself or those you love, you do yourself a disservice as a man and as a leader of your family. There are two main areas to learn: the rules of safety and the fundamentals of shooting.

Fundamentals of Shooting

The second part to being effective with a firearm is to know the fundamentals of shooting. These fundamentals are critical to having accurate shots and maximizing your ability to manage recoil. I have found that if you have a checklist to go over every time you prepare to shoot, you will not develop bad habits.

Shooting Fundamentals Checklist:

1. Stance
2. Grip
3. Sight Picture
4. Trigger Press
5. Follow Through

Stance – Ensure that your feet are shoulder-width apart, with the same foot as your dominant hand two inches back, your knees slightly bent with your hips back behind your shoulders.

Grip – Use your dominant hand to apply pressure like a vise front to back on the grip while your support hand is engaged applying pressure side to side.

Sight Picture – Concentrate on keeping your front sight aligned with your rear sight while focusing your attention on the target.

Trigger Press – Ease any slack out of the trigger, then steadily and gradually apply pressure until the firearm surprises you by firing.

Follow Through – Try to "call your shot" by remembering the sight picture right before the gun fires, assess your target through your sights and decide to fire again or not, take your finger off of the trigger, and look around for situational awareness.

I have fired over one million rounds in my life, yet, when I warm up, I still repeat this checklist aloud to cement the practice in my mind. With time, practice, and experience, this checklist will become second nature and will serve you as well as it has served me throughout my life.

If we travel back to that scrawny seven year old on the firing range, who used all his chore money to purchase ammunition and all his free time cleaning his gun, I wish I could tell him these things to make him into a firearms expert who didn't have to learn it the hard way. It amazes me to think that all this started for me through my first love, Victoria.

By the way Victoria was my first firearm, a beautiful Ruger Mark II .22 caliber pistol.

Guns in the Navy

When I joined the military, I essentially thought I would become a hired gun for justice, crushing the powers of darkness that threatened freedom, rescuing damsels in distress and what not. That was not the case. In Navy boot camp they gave us 1911-style .45 caliber pistols that had been re-bored to shoot .22 Long Rifle rounds. That was just a hair bigger than my pellet gun growing up. The vision I had of myself as a modern-day Wyatt Earp quickly faded. We only got to shoot about thirty rounds apiece, under threat of death if we screwed up, and then we were done. Over. I did not see a gun for more than two years after that. In hindsight, *not* giving us guns was probably an incredibly smart decision. After all, I was about thirty days out of being a huge pothead and one of the guys in my company told me in the follow-on Seaman Apprentice training that he smoked PCP on a regular basis for years before joining the Navy. This was back in 1988, so for those of you too young to know, PCP was the bath salts of that time.

Protecting California

Even during the first Gulf War, as I was guarding my tugboat in Northern California against the onslaught of Iraqi saboteurs that were planning to take over the Service Craft Division and wreak havoc on, well, nothing really, I was armed with only a radio to call no one and a pen. It is possible that I also had a flashlight. I figured that this would certainly change when I eventually shipped off to Commando School.

SEAL Training

It is very hard to understand BUD/S training unless you experience it firsthand. Most people envision Sailors running around killing crap all day long, but this is not the case at all. You do not even handle a weapon until you have been there for about four months, so it is a huge deal when you are finally issued a weapon as a SEAL trainee. You don't get any bullets, but, damn it, you have a gun. I remember seeing "upper class men," Third Phasers, with their fancy equipment and camouflage uniforms—but more importantly, weapons—and thinking that they had actually *made it*, and I was still a nobody. The build-up to getting a weapon is nearly overwhelming. Even more so in BUD/S training where everything is earned.

I don't recall if I even slept the night before getting my rifle in BUD/S, but I don't know how I could have. When the day finally arrived, it felt like Christmas morning as a young boy. You get up way before your parents—or in this case our third-phase instructors—and have to wait for them to have coffee before you can get to the good stuff. While your parents typically read you the Christmas story, at BUD/S it was an angry instructor reading you the riot act to not dick around with your gun. But eventually after all of that waiting and heavy anticipation, the magical moment finally arrives. You get to the head of the line and are handed black plastic and metal magic. This is done in a matter-of-fact manner. You step into the armory, they hand you your gun, they read off the serial number from a logbook as you verify it on the weapon, and you are done. I had anticipated possibly a short photo shoot, maybe a handshake, but received nothing other than: "Next!"

My first government-issued weapon was an M16 A1 with "HYDRA-MATIC DIV. G.M. Corp U.S.A." on the lower receiver.

The manufacturer name was confusing to me because I knew Colt made these weapons. After I started to ask around—remember this is pre-Internet days nearly—it turned out that during the Vietnam War many corporations made these guns. This meant there was a distinct possibility that the weapon I was given was *older than me*. The same company that made the Chevy Vega made my gun. The reason you probably never heard of that car is because it was straight junk. I was devastated. Here I was, nearly an actual SEAL, and they were providing me with a muzzle loader.

Thankfully, things were different when I got to my first SEAL Team. The armory was like Graceland to an Elvis fan or the Hormel Spam museum to a Pacific Islander. We had H&K P9Ses with sound suppressors, H&K MP-5s and MP-5 SDs, M14s, M60 E3s, M4s, Sig Sauer P226s, P228s, Smith & Wesson 686 stainless steel .357 revolvers, and one of my personal favorites: the Ruger MKII with a bull barrel and sound suppressor. I did not know that Larry's first gun was an MKII until I asked him to write his section of the book. Rounding this off, we also had the M203 and M79, both 40mm grenade launchers. The M203 was mounted under the barrel of the M4 and, as such, became an effective "weapons system."

I really liked the sound of that term and had many imaginary conversations with myself about this.

Them: "So, what kind of weapon do you carry?"

Me: "I don't carry a weapon, I carry a *weapons system*, pal."

These weapons were all designed for specific purposes. Some of them killed things loudly, and some killed things softly depending on what type of ammunition was used.

Ammunition

There are a zillion types of ammunition, so I will only write about a few, or this will just get confusing.

The standard NATO rounds for rifles are the 7.62x51mm and the 5.56x45mm, and for the pistol ammunition, the 9mm Parabellum. That is the "9" jackass gangsters talk about regularly. The AK-47 shoots a 7.62x39mm in case you were wondering.

Shotguns use something called a "shell" even though it is not the former home of a sea creature. Shotgun shells are much larger than a bullet you would normally use for anything other than hunting for a truck or tank or shooting from a plane. I am assuming you guys are not going to be doing this, so we will skip those. A shotgun shell differs from a regular bullet not only in size but also in composition. Most are about two and three-quarters inches to three and a half inches of plastic with just the bottom being made of metal. They have a bunch of little BBs, called "shot," in them that spread out after they leave the barrel. They come in different sizes, from ten- to twenty-gauge; unlike other ammunition, the larger the number, the smaller the size. There is also another number associated with the shell that tells you the size and roughly the amount of these BBs in the shell. They go from #2 to #9 shot. Again, the smaller the number, the larger the shot, but the fewer that are in there. There are also things called "buckshot" and "slugs." The buckshot has the largest size shot in it of a shell with more than one projectile in it. The slug is a single, very large piece of lead or other material, very similar to an old-school musket ball.

What's the Difference?

The 5.56 or .223 round is what you think of when you think of an M16. There is actually a significant difference in these bullets, but, for the sake of what we are speaking about, this difference is nominal. Both of these rounds are teeny .22 caliber bullets. What makes this unique is that it's hauling ass so fast, and when it hits you within fourteen inches it spins over and causes a huge *temporary cavity*, also called "temporary cavitation," that is very large in proportion to the round. Once that temporary cavity collapses you have a *permanent cavity*. This is what you see if you see a "bullet hole" in someone.

This cavitation is a result of energy being transferred from the bullet to flesh. The flesh expands like a balloon blowing up inside of your leg. As it does, the bullet devitalizes all that tissue, so it breaks all the little blood vessels and shreds other tissue. Even though it looks like there's a tiny hole where the bullet entered, there's a swath that goes through that tissue that is wrecked. The exit wounds are normally much larger and rather graphic. Google "ballistic gel" and you will see what that looks like inside your body. All of that flesh has to be cut out, or it will die. This same mechanism takes place with all high-powered ammunition.

Bows and Arrows

And here we are again, something potentially dangerous, so I have to spend more time pointing out the obvious because of my lawyer who I am sure is bubble-wrapped out of fear of scraping his knee. In case you have never heard of a "bow and arrow" when used separately or together, they can be downright dangerous. Ninja damn dangerous. Do not shoot an arrow directly up in the air and then run away; it will not turn out well for you and your friends. Do not put an apple or any other type of fruit, or really anything, on your friend's head and try to shoot it off. Do not use arrows to clean your teeth. If you want to learn how to shoot these great weapons safely, do something more than read this book. Go to an outdoor store that sells these things and ask someone there where you can take some lessons.

This is one of those skills I figured it'd be better to have someone who is a master explain, so I asked my friend Jody Neal. Jody is a very interesting cat, stands about six foot four, and is what is known as a *kyoshi* or a master of karate. I like to call him "karaoke". That is a master of annoying people in a bar after drinking too much. I met Jody on an executive retreat where we shot a little bit and hiked around in the desert. It's something that we do periodically, and I think it has great value, both for me to understand what it's like to be a business executive, and for them to talk to people that view the world from a very different perspective. We are also fun to hang out with and drink some beers with around the campfire.

Once Jody and I started talking, I realized that even though he wasn't a SEAL, he truly was a martial artist. Until that point, I had never thought about the meaning of the term "martial arts." We became fast friends and, as a matter of fact, we stayed up all night going through our backpacks and comparing survival gear. By the way, he had much more than I did. As a matter of fact, he had *way, way* more than he needed, because we were staying right next to a house. However, if you were to drop Jody in the middle of the Atlantic Ocean in February, he would have been fine.

Getting to know him on the retreat, I realized that we had a lot in common. He's a father, a professional, a man of faith, and took his job very seriously. But I never really know whether someone knows what they are talking about until I test them.

"Okay, Mr. Karate-Master-Karaoke, what's the coolest thing you've ever done with a bow and arrow?" I asked.

He went on to explain that he had pulled off what is known as a "Robin Hood," meaning he shot one arrow into a target and then shot a second arrow into the back of that arrow, which is fairly impressive.

Then I looked him square in the eyes. "I'm going to ask you one question. If you answer this question correctly, I will believe that you are who you say you are. If not, you're just a liar. Could you, in fact, beat Ralph Macchio, also known as Daniel LaRusso, in a karate fight?"

Jody looked at me and honestly said, "Of course not. That crane maneuver—it cannot be defeated."

And that is when I knew Jody was, in fact, a kyoshi, a master of masters of karate.

Another reason I consider Jody a man is that he has a tremendous heart for giving. A couple of years ago, he came up with an idea to start an orphanage. I think a lot of people have thought of these fantastic ideas, but the difference between a male and a man is that a man actually acts on it. Jody asked me to help him do this, and we started what's known as the Alpha Project Americas. Alpha Project is designed to help break the cycle of poverty in third-world countries, and the only way to really do it effectively is to have it be long-lasting. This means teaching important skills to children, starting with the younger generations, so, as they grow, they'll have an understanding and a respect for labor, not just labor, but work. This will be done by teaching then hard skills: plumbing, carpentry, and electrical work. They'll have dignity knowing that they can have a positive effect on the world. From having dignity, they will grow into honorable men.

The Alpha Project will be kicking off in Costa Rica. This is something that we've done together, and it's something that made me respect Jody even more.

How to Shoot an Arrow With a Bow

By Jody Neal

Jody Neal

5th Degree Black Belt and honorary title, kyoshi in Shaolin Kempo. Opened, owned, or operated thirteen studios in three states.

Founder of the Alpha Project, a non-profit foundation for children. *www.alphaprojectamericas.org*

Skills and hobbies: archery, fishing, firearms, carpentry, tile, basketball, camping, cooking, mentoring, building/fixing nearly anything mechanical, and backhanded compliments.

Second only to firearms in power, range, and effectiveness as a projectile kinetic weapon, the bow and arrow is a silent and cost-effective way to become a better marksman. It is also an excellent hunting tool. And now that girls do it in the movies, it's an easy sell to your wife to set up an archery range in the back yard (as opposed to a pistol course). There are two common types of bows: recurve and compound. There are "purists" who will tell you that it requires more skill to operate a recurve and, therefore, it's better. While I will acknowledge it does require more skill, so does shooting with a flintlock musket. So as soon as Navy SEALs start conducting operations with flintlocks and swords, I'll start using a recurve bow. In the meantime, I'll keep using an ultra-high-tech carbon-fiber compound bow with fiber-optic sights. If you happen to discover that you have a talent for archery and somebody wants to take you down a notch by telling you that you're "cheating" by using high-tech equipment, politely suggest they go beat Tiger in a round of golf by using golf clubs from the 1940s. It is the same logic.

The technique I will describe below is a hybrid of Eastern and Western archery techniques. I like to descend my sights onto the target. It's easier to stay on target by lowering the bow than lifting it. It assumes a right-handed archer.

1. Fix the nock, have the arrow on to the string, and attach the trigger.

2. Stand sideways to the target with your feet approximately eighteen inches apart.

3. Look at the target with both eyes open with the bow down at your waist.

4. Lift the bow above your head with the grip slightly in front of your left shoulder.

5. Take note of your breath and all of your body from foot to head, then inhale.

6. Bring the bow down and push with your left hand while pulling with your right.

7. Drawing the string back fully, put the string across the tip of your nose while your right eye sees the target through the peep sight on the string. Make sure you are exhaling the whole time.

8. Keeping, both eyes open (my preference) lower the sight onto the target (still on the exhale).

9. Relax your grip on the left hand so you are only pushing opposite the draw, not squeezing the grip.

10. When you have the sight precisely where you want it, release the trigger by subtly dropping your index finger. There should be no other detectable movement.

11. As the arrow is released, allow the bow to fall naturally. But make sure you don't just drop it.

12. Repeat with two more arrows (if your group is tight, more than three arrows starts wrecking fletchings and nocks)

Tips: (1) Stay relaxed; tension makes it hard to stay consistent. (2) Learn to breathe and control your heart rate. You can actually learn to shoot between heartbeats. (3) All of the same safety rules apply to an archery range as a firearms range except ear and eye protection.

Jody Neal
Executive Director
Alpha Project International
3433 State Street, Suite A
Santa Barbara, CA 93105
(844) ALPHA 74

Making a Fist

My cousin Damien Roth and I grew up together for a couple of years. Something interesting about Damien is that he's a pretty quiet, thoughtful person, but he's also been doing full-contact fighting for over a dozen years now. For those of you unfamiliar with what this is, it's called mixed martial arts, and these guys are actual warriors. They are truly fighting in the most brutal fashion possible. It is a test of wills. You can really tell that this sport is something unique by the fact that even the greats have been beaten, because at some point your body can only take so much damage.

The ability of these fighters to move from standing and striking positions to on-the-ground grappling, all within the rules of the sport, is what makes it exciting to watch and so dangerous to participate in. I wanted Damien to be in this book not because of his ability to fight, but because he has come to mean something very much to me by the way he has faced a very difficult time in his life.

Damien's daughter Lucy was diagnosed with brain cancer and has been treated several times with radiation, surgeries, and all the things that you do to get rid of the horrific disease. Throughout the years of treatment, Damien has remained strong. To see your child sick or injured is one of the most difficult things that any parent can ever face. Flesh of your flesh, blood of your blood. It is incredibly heartwrenching to see this happen. But Damien has been staying the course for years now, as has Lucy. This is part of the essence of being a man, understanding that there are people that you care about who are truly in pain and who are hurting, are confused, and who are scared, but you stand strong. You stand tall and you stand with them. That's what we are called to do.

Leadership, at its essence, is providing an environment where people can thrive. This is what Damien has been doing for his daughter Lucy, and that makes him a true man. It is not the fact that he can knock the crap out of you, which he can. It's the fact that he stands strong every day for his daughter, and the rest of his family, and continues to march on. And that is why I have tremendous respect for him.

Putting Your Best Fist Forward

By Damien Roth

I am a fight geek, or fight savant, if you will. I am infatuated with hand-to-hand combat in any and all of its glorious forms, and I share this with you without any hint of guilt or embarrassment. My infatuation began many years ago, nurtured by my grandfather, a WWII veteran and patriotic John Wayne fan. You could say I never really had a chance. It began with *Big Jake* and *Rio Lobo*, our two all-time favorite Westerns, and continued on with a steady diet of professional wrestling, *The Rockford Files*, Charlie Bronson, Burt Reynolds, and, of course, the man himself, Clint Eastwood. I mean, who didn't want to be one of these men at some point, right? It was just simple logic to me.

I have since gone on to study a number of martial arts including Kodokon Judo, Brazilian Jiu-Jitsu, boxing, MMA, and Muay Thai. I have thrown and absorbed literally thousands of punches. Over my twenty-plus years of training, I've learning how to both receive and occasionally deliver a proper beating. Through great trial and error, I have come to one universal conclusion: Giving a beating is much more gratifying than being on the receiving end.

Making a proper fist is a beautiful thing, in both its simplicity and effectiveness. It is also an essential tool that every young man should possess in the event he should ever need it. First, you curl your four fingers and tuck them into the palm as if you were grabbing a rope. You then wrap your thumb down and around the outside of your index finger, allowing the thumb tip to finally come to rest on the middle finger. Do not wrap your thumb into the palm with your fingers, and, by all means, don't leave the thumb hanging out. Both of these mistakes can cause great injury to the ligaments and muscles of the hand. With the thumb tucked in under the fingers, upon impact, the joint at the base of the thumb will most likely absorb a great amount of energy, thus resulting in damage. The thumb hanging out, in my opinion, is worse yet because it can become hooked or tangled en route to its intended target, resulting in damage not only to the joint but also to the supporting muscle, as well as the wrist. This is why any decent pair of boxing gloves possess both a padded bar in the palm to clamp your grip down on and an attached thumb to prevent it from becoming caught or hung up.

It is imperative to have your gift properly packed before sending it down range to its intended recipient.

Once the proper mechanics have been applied, take careful aim and fire away. This is where the real fun begins!

The Lucy Jane Roth Medical Fund has been established at Bank of the West. Donors may stop by their local branch or send checks to help with Lucy's current and future medical expenses. If you do not have a Bank of the West near you, you can still donate by doing the following:

Make check payable to:
Lucy Jane Roth Medical Fund

NOTE: It is important to endorse the back of the check if you are mailing!

Endorse the back of the check with:
For Deposit Only
Lucy Jane Roth Medical Fund

Mail check to: Bank of the West
800 22nd Avenue
Coralville, IA 52241

Punching

I asked Jody to pen this part also specifically because he is not a SEAL and earns his keep by teaching people this skill. The thought to include his "Step 5" would never occur to a SEAL.

But, before we get into something actually entertaining and helpful, here is another disclaimer courtesy of my uptight lawyer. I am going to share his note with you verbatim: "A disclaimer needs to be added about only using a punch in self-defense or something like that. Otherwise, you are literally teaching someone how to commit the tort of battery, or worse."

I had no idea I was teaching someone a tort of anything. I thought that was a pastry. I don't even think this guy read the section. We are talking about hitting someone in the face with a fist, not a doughnut. If you find yourself in a position where you need to defend yourself or someone else, do it properly. If you use these skills to randomly beat up people or bully them, you are so far removed from manhood, you need to do some real soul-searching. So, no battered torts.

If you are in California and want to learn how to punch properly, visit one of Jody's studios. If you are in Minnesota or western Wisconsin, come in and see Larry Yatch at Sealed Mindset. They do great scenario-based self-defense training, with and without firearms.

How to Deliver a Punch

By Jody Neal

United Studios of
SELF DEFENSE

There are five hundred different ways to deliver a knockout blow, and every know-it-all on earth with tell you something different. I have trained literally thousands of people in the proper mechanics of punching. You can throw a John Wayne haymaker, a Mike Tyson uppercut, or a nasty sucker punch. However, if you want the punch to be effective, there are only three rules: 1) The punch must be on target. In order render an ass-clown unconscious, you need to shake his brain like Jell-O. Attacking the jaw at a forty-five-degree angle is the best way. 2) It must be a ferocious blow. You have to generate enough kinetic force to rotate the head so quickly that the brain stays still in the core but twists on the outer part. 3) Last and most importantly, you have to overcome every instinct and chemical signal in your body that is telling you there is more danger in clocking this guy than standing there and taking a beating from him. That's the hardest part. But if you remember when Ralphie from *A Christmas Story* decked Scut Farkus, you know that changing the rules on a bully turns the tables. You have to become a predator instead of prey.

1. Make a fist.
2. Locate the target.
3. Steel your nerve.
4. Punch hard in a straight line from your dominant hand across and through target. Keep your fist with the thumb on the topside like you're holding a bouquet of flowers and handing them really hard through the jaw.
5. Call your lawyer.

Jody Neal
Godan (5th Degree Black Belt)
United Studio of Self Defense

Central Coast, California
www.centralcoastussd.com

Knives, the Other Weapons

Another weapon you can get that reflects that fact you're growing into manhood is a knife. Not a kitchen knife but a real knife, like a folding pocketknife. The chances of you having a knife and never cutting yourself with one are zero, so be prepared for that. Having a knife and having it dull is just like having a weapon and having it not sighted in. Regardless, any knife that you have should be sharp.

Yeah! Lawyer time! At no time should you poke yourself in the eye with a knife, or a pencil, or a paper clip. Or, sand. I just put eye drops in my eyes, that is okay, that is why they call them "eye drops." Be careful with your knives, or you will be spending some time in the emergency room.

When I was in BUD/S training, they used to give us the MK 3 Mod 0 K-Bar, pronounced "Mark three Mod O." It was the "official Navy SEAL knife" and happened to be the world's largest piece of crap knife ever. I have no idea where they got the steel for making these things, but it was just pathetic. I had a friend named Rick who once had his knife in the scabbard, which is a sheath for the blade that is made of plastic with a little metal clip that held the knife in place. We went swimming in the ocean...with our knifes, as you do. When he pulled it out, the blade actually broke off and stayed in the scabbard as he pulled the handle out. They were that poorly made.

It was nearly impossible to get these knives to keep an edge. You would sharpen them and it seemed like they would get dull as you were putting them away. When we were in BUD/S, the first weapon knife-sharpening systems came out, and one model was by Lansky™. It had fixed angles that you would run the blade on and different levels of grit in order to sharpen it. It would start with that coarser grit and then slowly work its way to a finer grit. My roommate, Rob, who is still one of my best friends ever, was a parachute rigger, meaning he was responsible for folding up the parachutes in the proper way so that when you jumped out of an aircraft, they would open and you wouldn't die. Rob, being the stickler for detail that he was, purchased this Lansky knife-sharpening system, and his Mark 3 Mod 0 was like a lightsaber, it was so sharp. Luke Skywalker would have been proud to have this thing.

Prior to any water evolution (that is a fancy name for an "event") in BUD/S, you do what's called a "swimmer inspection." You'd stand with your small CO_2 cartridge in one hand that would go into your life vest and your knife in the other. The instructors would come by to make sure that your CO2 cartridge was clean, polished, and that there wasn't a hole poked in the bottom of it, meaning it hadn't been actuated yet and it would still function. Then, they would pick up your knife and check it to make sure it was sharp and not at all rusty. Of course, no one's knives were particularly sharp because they're such pieces of crap. However, as we know, Robert's was.

One of the instructors was walking by—he happened to be a corpsman—and he was picking up people's knives and feeling the edges, and they're obviously dull. He'd throw them into the surf zone or bang them on a rock on a beach while he yelled at everybody for not taking care of their equipment. As the instructor moved his way down the line, he finally got to Robert. By this time he was nearly in a rage, and he picked up Robert's knife and did something you should never do. He rubbed his thumb right along the blade of the knife to prove that this knife was not sharp. Unfortunately for him, as we know, Robert's knife was, in fact, a surgical instrument, and he sliced his thumb open.

As a BUD/S instructor, he was, by definition, a rather tough guy, and being a corpsman, means that he knew first aid. Well, this corpsman looked at his thumb and saw that it was gashed open and would require several stitches. Then he looked at Robert. He handed Robert his knife back and said, "Nice knife." Then he turned and walked away and got his thumb sewn up.

When something like this happens in BUD/S, you really never know if you're able to laugh. You're obviously *able* to laugh, but you don't know if you *should* laugh because there is a guy in front of you who is your superior both in rank and experience. He has something you don't, in this case a Trident. However, he does something that is so goofy, you really want to laugh, but you are afraid that if you laugh you'll spend the rest of your day in the surf zone.

So we quietly chuckled to ourselves and carried on.

How to Sharpen a Knife

The guy I've asked to explain how to sharpen a knife is named Brian Montgomery, and he has been a friend of mine since high school. Granted, I didn't spend a lot of time in high school, but I still got to know several guys very well. Brian was always the guy that was one step above the rest, composed, but still crazy enough to be fun. He works for a company now called Benchmade™, which, in my opinion, manufactures the finest knives in the entire world, and he is in charge of military and government sales. I didn't know this until a little while ago when we reconnected after several years of me being in the Navy and dropping off the radar. I had a chance to tour the factory where they make these knives with pride. It was utterly impressive, an absolute demonstration of American ingenuity and know-how.

Keep Your Tool Sharp

By Brian Montgomery

How do you sharpen a knife? Well, let's back up. First of all, you must make a decision to carry a knife. There are a number of reasons why, and I am frequently asked with some degree of incredulity: "Why do you always carry a knife?"

What? How could you even consider *not* carrying a knife? There are a number of utilitarian uses, not the least of which is personal defense. But, I digress. Let's assume you've made that decision (good for you!). Now, let's briefly discuss selection.

Take your time in picking the right one (or several) for you and your EDC (that's Every Day Carry) needs. Now, that knife will need some maintenance. It will get dull over time and accumulate dirt, grime, lint, and other foreign matter. A drop of lube in the action (pivot point) and some general cleaning should suffice to keep it moving smoothly.

As for keeping it sharp, start with the honing stick in your kitchen knife block or drawer. This will keep the edge straight, but not actually sharpen it. For that you'll need a stone—either a flat one or round. Typically, they are ceramic, occasionally diamond-encrusted, and will all do the job.

Look at the edge of your knife and determine the approximate angle at which it was ground when manufactured. You will want to follow that angle as you slowly and evenly move the blade across the stone. Smoothly is the key. If you feel your grip or angle slipping or changing, just stop and begin again. You can't put material back on the edge, but you can correct the angle if you stop.

Just repeat on the other side.

In a pinch, you could even use an inverted coffee cup if the edge on the bottom is raised and free of any glazing. It is ceramic material similar to a sharpening stone. Again, slowly and smoothly.

If you want to be really high speed, buy a Benchmade® knife (easily the highest quality and coolest production knives on the market), and when it needs maintenance, just send it in to the company. They will repair, maintain, and sharpen your knife for free for the life of the knife.

Good luck and stay sharp.

You Be the Judge

When I was going to school in San Antonio, Texas with the Army Special Forces Medical Sergeants Course, we used to be able to walk on and off the military base very easily. As a matter of fact, the only gate that was there was the road, meaning the chain-link fence next to the building that we trained in. There wasn't even anyone there watching it.

A lady named Alma owned a house right on the other side of the chain-link fence and, being an industrious American, she built her garage into a bar. It was a place we would frequent after work and get together to drink beer. One night while we were out getting liquored up, I noticed there was a colonel from the British SAS and his sergeant major sitting at the bar. I was kind of fascinated by this because I had never met a guy from the SAS. I was talking to these guys, listening to their stories, and they were enjoying having a young American serviceman listen to them, so they're getting all British. At this time I didn't have my Trident. Although I had graduated from BUD/S, I wasn't a qualified SEAL yet.

At one point, some guys started getting into a scuffle in the back of Alma's place near the pool table and two of them happened to be my friends. They soon walked by where I was sitting and said they were going to go outside and get in a fight with a few Army guys. Without hesitating, I said I would go with them.

I started walking in front of my friends with the Army guys right in front of me, him and his two buddies. They walked out of Alma's place, and I just closed the door behind them, and then we went back in and I kept drinking beer with the SAS guys. Now Alma wouldn't let them back in because they were not attached to a Special Forces unit. They were just regular, straight-stick Army guys from the other side of the base.

So we sat there and drank beer for a while, me hearing stories about how great England is and how they saved the world repeatedly and everything else. And then at about two o'clock in the morning, Alma decided to close up for the night. My two buddies and I walked outside of the bar.

Even though it had been three or four hours since I last saw them, the Army guys were still outside. And there weren't only three of them as there had been earlier—there were now four. Apparently, they'd been sitting out there building up courage while we had been inside drinking. The first Army guy that came up and talked to me was the one who originally wanted to get into a fight with my friends inside earlier.

"Look, Pal, we're just going to go ahead and leave," I told him. "We're just leaving."

He was a big tall guy, probably around six foot three, and he had no interest in listening to anything I had to say. He was standing on a curb in front of me, yelling, insulting my manhood, and telling me that I committed sexual acts with other men and whatnot. You can fill in the blanks. Anyway, I had no intention of standing out in front of the bar all night.

"Hey, man, we're just going to go ahead and leave," I said.

"Bullshit you're not going to leave," he yelled. At that point, he started to move his hand forward like he was going to push me. Without hesitation, I made a proper fist, and I threw a punch, a straight uppercut in this instance, and I hit him right on the tip of his chin.

Unfortunately, my hand slipped off of his chin and two of his teeth stuck into my knuckles. As I pulled my hand away, he fell unconscious to the sidewalk. I immediately saw movement to my right and turned as one of his buddies was trying to jump on my back. But as soon as he saw his friend knocked out on the ground, he turned around and ran away. A real life two-birds-with-one-stone situation just went down.

Unfortunately, it wasn't much fun pulling the teeth out of my knuckles. In fact, when I went back to school after the weekend, I had to talk to the doctor who was in charge of the course because my hand was getting infected. When he asked me what happened to my hand, I told him I had cut it when I fell on it running. As soon as he looked at it and realized I was right-handed, he knew that I was lying.

And there you have it.

Wrap Up on Weapons and Violence in General

As a civilian, it should always be the exception to get into a fight, unless you are a student of martial arts or a professional fighter. As a member of the military, you should dedicate your life to winning fights. At the end of the day, that is what you are getting paid for. I neither glorify violence nor condemn it because it is a tool to be used to achieve a goal. The purpose of that goal is what determines if the violence should have been used or not. People who say violence never solved anything are simply delusional. People who say violence is the only solution are just as whacked. Sometimes you have to defend yourself and, if you can, other people. That is what a man chooses to do, and, yes, once again, you must make that choice.

CHAPTER III

Outdoor Skills

Many years ago in our country if a man was fully capable of living outdoors for long periods of time he was called an "explorer." Now, when people live outdoors they are called hobos or bums, and they certainly aren't respected. Or, they are called "preppers." These are the folks who are preparing for the imminent destruction of the world. Oftentimes, they can be spotted by the aluminum hats they often wear to keep out the signals from the Government Office of Crazypants Broadcasting. People say that you should expect the unexpected, but I think this is goofy. Does this mean that I should expect to be hit in the head with an asteroid being ridden by a drug-crazed nun wearing a sombrero she stole from Pancho Villa's tomb? I can't think of anything more unexpected than that.

SEALs expect the expected. That is why it is called "the expected." We also plan on having to deal with the worst situations that may arise. I bring this up because sometimes we can lose focus on reality and work ourselves into a dither. Around town that is generally okay, but in the great outdoors, it can kill you.

To be a man, not only is it important that you be able to operate any piece of equipment that you come into contact with, but you should also be able to survive and thrive while living outdoors, within reason.

One of the basics when we talk about thriving in the wilderness is very much like what they say in real estate, "It's all about location, location, location."

Depending on the climate you're in, you obviously need to bring different types of equipment. If you're going to live in the jungle, you must understand that there are several types of jungle, and whatever type of jungle you go into will dictate what you bring. For instance, the country of Panama is absolutely the gnarliest place I have ever been in my life. There are *Bactris* palms and many other types of plants that have spikes which can range from one to five inches in length. These barbs are so sharp they will go right through your leather boots and embed in your skin. Generally speaking in Panama, everything there is specifically designed to kill you, make you itch, give you a rash, or have your face swell up. When I was at SEAL Team FOUR, I spent five years in and around South and Central America jungles where there were nasty mosquitoes, vampire bats, and saturniid caterpillars, which look kind of like small, very hairy dogs, or even like worms festooned with television antennas from the 1950s. These strange, little creatures can sting you and send you into anaphylactic shock.

There is an odd phenomenon with creatures like the saturniid caterpillar and many poisonous snakes. They tend to strike mostly men on their dominant hands, often their index fingers. No one really knows why this is. I have personally treated a Navy SEAL who was apparently minding his own business when one of these incredibly fascinating-looking creatures snuck up on him, removed the glove from his right hand, and then stung him right on the tip of his index finger.

There are some jungles that are definitely more mild than others. At one point in my career, I had the opportunity to go to New Zealand to train with some of their guys. When I went, I packed up two full flyer's kit bags, which are the size of a large suitcase, with every piece of protective equipment I could imagine. I had about a gallon of "bug juice," also known as insect repellent, as well as items like gloves, boots, beekeeper head nets, and my hammock that had mosquito netting built in. Basically, I was ready for war.

When I showed up in New Zealand and started going through my equipment before going into the field, I noticed the Kiwis flashing me some odd looks.

"What's all this stuff for, mate?" One of them asked.

"Well, we're going to go live in the jungle," I told him.

My response prompted more looks from the guys, but at the time I didn't know what the issue was. We were preparing to go into the jungle for six weeks, and I wanted to be prepared. I didn't understand their reactions until we actually found ourselves out in the jungle, or *bush* as they call it. During our entire trip, I think I saw a grand total of *four* mosquitoes in New Zealand. In fact, at night, you can actually lie down on the ground and sleep with sugar on your face, and when you wake up, you will just have a sticky face. I think the Kiwis thought I wore an aluminum hat at home.

This was opposed to Panama where a group of guys from Hotel Platoon at SEAL Team FOUR thought they were going to be really cool and, instead of sleeping in their hammocks, they slept on the ground. Four of them ended up being bitten by vampire bats. Vampire bats. That is just fun to write.

Needless to say, each environment carries its own dangers, but I have found some of these to also be part of the rewarding experience of spending time there. Often, the more spectacular the jungle, the cooler the elements you will discover in it.

Over the course of my career, I have been to survival schools in Panama, the Philippines, Malaysia, and, my personal favorite, Survival Evasion Resistance and Escape (SERE) school right here in America. If you have been to SERE school, you realize that was a joke. I would rather run my face over a cheese grater then go there again. I don't remember much about the school in Panama other than I was a new guy at the time, we were on deployment, and it was more of a jungle familiarization than how to survive in the jungle. The school in the Philippines called Jungle Environmental Survival Training (JEST) was much more involved. Our lead instructor was a native Filipino named Joseph, who, at the time, was in his seventies. When he was a child, the Japanese invaded, and his father took him and the rest of his family into the jungle where they lived during the entire occupation. He was a walking encyclopedia of history and knowledge.

I found out that this school was intergenerational when I returned from this deployment and went on vacation with my family. During our trip, we visited my Uncle Bob. As it turns out, Bob was on his way to Laos in 1962 at the behest of the same fish chowder-loving President Kennedy that created the SEAL Teams. As a part of the Marines' pre-deployment training, they attended JEST where Uncle Bob had an instructor named Joseph. What kind of crazy is that?

Joseph was about five foot nothing and a straight-up badass. Prior to getting into the real training, he took us on a walk where he showed us how to make everything but a Predator drone with stuff he picked up along the trail. Things that you don't realize that you need until you need them. Like rope from bark and cooking utensils. As I am the curious type, I was walking directly behind Joseph when he quickly shot his hand out as fast as lightning into a tree. I am telling you, Keanu Reeves in *The Matrix* did not move this fast. I froze in place as he spun around to face the rest of the SEALs and me. Joseph calmly held the emerald green serpent six inches in front of my face. I have never been afraid of snakes, but I have always respected them.

"Baam-boo viper," he said plainly and without a hint of excitement.

In Joseph's hand was what is known as the "three-step snake" or more accurately the bamboo viper. It was called the three-step snake because, if you were bitten, you supposedly could take only three steps before you died. This is a bit of an exaggeration, but, nonetheless, this species is very lethal. After showing me the snake, Joseph went to the next SEAL and repeated: "Baam-boo viper," and so on down the line. When he got to the last SEAL, Joseph walked back to the front of the patrol where I was standing. He casually threw the deadly snake on the ground and then stepped on it with his flip-flop, killing it instantly. It was surreal.

We were sixteen Navy SEALs with guns, knives, great hair and attitudes, and here was a seventy-something-year-old midget who kills death itself with his sandal. I won't say this was discouraging, but, at the same time, I felt just a bit smaller.

As I mentioned, I also attended Survival Evasion Resistance and Escape school in America, which is also nicknamed "Crap, I hate this place." Officially, it is Code of Conduct training and deserves a heck of a lot more attention that I am going to pay it here. Most people go through SERE training as newer pilots or, if they are SEALs or Special Forces Soldiers, as new guys, meaning they have a bunch of training as SEALs or SF, but no experience.

When I attended, I had been a SEAL for six years had done two platoons and three deployments, one to Bosnia immediately following the Dayton Accords, so I was not a new guy. To be honest, I thought the whole thing was going to be rather silly. The purpose is to learn basic food scavenging and survival methods. You start out with very little in the way of gear. By this, I mean no knives, guns, warm clothing, fire-starting equipment, etc. When I asked why we essentially had nothing with us, the SERE instructor said we were practicing worst-case scenario. Again, I thought this was a bit much as, when I was in the field, I had multiple guns, knives, grenades, and assorted survival gear—including the most useful tool of all: a Visa card and some Benjamins, just in case they only took American Express. The only scenario that I could envision where I did not have all of this stuff was if I were somehow magically transported from the shower directly into enemy territory. As this was unlikely, I have to admit that I was not the star pupil.

What I learned in SERE school was that I could walk around for a long time and be hungry. I had actually learned that before, so I guess it was just a good reminder. The important thing to note is that each environment has challenges. You should do your homework prior to getting yourself into a situation that you are not sure how to get out of. There is no substitute for local knowledge when it comes to these matters, so seek out an expert from the region.

Desert

For the record, I hate the desert. I'm not going to pretend like I like it. Not only is it hot and dusty, but also the food is generally awful...unless you like to eat goat. Or camel. I like goat, but not enough to compensate for the rest of the hassles involved with the desert. I would rather get into a hand-clapping competition to the death with a North Korean than eat another camel. Think about that for a minute. In fact, I have dry eyes now because of the desert. Apparently, the intense heat burnt up my tear ducts. What kind of crap is that? Whether it was for training purposes or deployed in combat, I spent conservatively nine straight years in the desert. Whenever you are out in an environment such as this, you have to be prepared to carry all of the water you think you might consume for the entire time you are there. I don't mean you need to carry four thousand bottles of water for your vacation to Las Vegas; I am referring to if you are heading out for a hike or a camping trip.

What is the one thing everyone knows about the desert? It is very hot. But what is often overlooked is just how cold it can become at night, relatively speaking, meaning it can get up to 120+ degrees during the day, like it regularly did when I spent time in Africa, and then down to 60 degrees at night. You would think you'd still be warm, but the sixty-degree temperature differential was tough to adapt to, and you're actually jackhammering freezing. To compensate for this, and just like anything, you must be prepared. The first things to do in order are: 1) Get the hell out, 2) find water, 3) make shelter, and 4) make fire. As this is not a survival manual, we will skip to number 4.

How to Make Fire and Influence People

It is said that the ability to start a fire is what separates humans from the other primates. In my opinion, it is the corn-dog. Somewhere out there, there must be a chimp that can produce flame. There has to be, but you can bet your ass none of those dudes can make a corn dog. Corn dogs are one of the greatest inventions of all time, if not *the* greatest. I have no idea why this is but decided years ago not to question this magnificent and eternal truth. With that said, making fire is fantastic. It provides heat and light, and, when you are outdoors for any period of time, entertainment. Many of the SEALs I know call it "God's television" while Army guys call it "Ranger television." I will not comment on this since I am pretty sure that God does not have a television, and I would hate to admit an Army guy was right.

As a result of my extensive training, I can whip fire up with a bowstring and wood shavings as well as flint and steel. I can make it from uniquely cut and shaped bamboo, a magnifying glass, magnesium, and other assorted things. In short, if I were inclined, I would be a fantastic pyromaniac.

However, I am not going to show you folks how to make a fire with all of the "primitive" stuff because, today, the "primitive" stuff costs a lot of money and is rather silly. I am sure that I just made some prepper's list of death again, but at least I know I will be warm when they attack me with a throwing star made from the lid of a Spam can.

It never occurred to me that, with all of this crazy training we receive as SEALs, no one ever taught us how to make a fire with matches...or a lighter. Never. This is just something I picked up along the way.

This became painfully apparent in 1995 while I was on a training trip to the country of Chile. They named it "Chile" but they actually meant to call it "chilly", because it was freezing! It is a beautiful country, very Castilian, European. We were training with our counterparts, and then a couple of weeks in, we were given the weekend off. We being the outdoor type, and due to the fact that we were in a remote place in the off season, there was not much else to do but go hiking up a small but impressive mountain. Being SEALs, we packed everything necessary for the hike: several bottles of the local wine, some Meals Ready to Eat (MREs), and cameras to document our expedition.

When the five of us finally reached the top, we had crossed into the clouds, and it became rather cold. I told the guys to start a fire and wandered off not thinking much about it. When I returned about fifteen minutes later, every one of them was standing around looking uncomfortable. They started looking at the ground and shuffling their feet when I asked why they had not started a fire. And then it hit me: four hairy-chested Freedom Fighting Frogmen did not know how to start a fire *with* the matches provided in the MREs we brought. And that, dear friends, is why I will now show you.

The key to making a fire is preparation. By this, I mean either being in a place where you want to have to make a fire and having all the stuff to make a fire or not getting into a place where you need a fire but don't have anything to make it with. We're going to go with the former here. As I explained, this isn't going to be anything fancy. We're not going to use flint, bamboo, or one of those exotic bows. We're just going to use some good old-fashioned matches.

There are a couple of different kinds of matches. One is called "farmer's matches," which you can light by striking on any rough surface. There's a little point on the tip, and it ignites with friction, causing the rest of the match to burn. The other match type is probably one you are more familiar with. They typically come in a box or packet, and are often made of wood or paper. Either way, you have to scratch these along a type of grit that's attached to the box or the pack of matches, similar to an emery board that you would file your nails with. You may find it disturbing that a SEAL knew that was called an emery board. I don't know how I feel about it myself.

You want to go from small to big when making a fire, and the goal is to have to use only one match. Initially, find some very small material, either sticks or leaves, and set those aside. If the ground is damp, try removing the top layer of the leaves and other material underneath. Unless you are in a rain-soaked jungle, this area under the surface should be moderately dry. Next, grab your sticks and leaves, and start breaking these things into little two-inch pieces or small balls of leaves. You want to form a pyramid, like a teepee, with these sticks, putting the crunched-up dried leaves or grass underneath. If you are going to use grass, twist it together, forming something that looks sort of like rope because it will burn for a longer period of time than if it remains loose.

Once you have the little sticks in a teepee, find some larger sticks, and make those into a teepee over the top of the ones you just put down. Keep doing this until you have three layers of sticks that get progressively bigger as they go out from the center of the teepee. You should also have other firewood standing by because, once this burns, you will have a small base of coals that you can put larger sticks on. When I say "larger," I mean probably two and a half to three inches square or round, depending on whether or not they're chopped or cut.

Now it's time to take out your match. You want to light it, and put it at the very base of the teepee either under the curled-up grass or the bunched-up leaves. The flame should catch rapidly and move upward. If it burns but then goes out and there's still little embers, you can blow on the material in order to make it flame up. I caution you not to blow too hard or too fast, or you might hyperventilate and pass out, burying your face in the fire. Granted, that would be really funny; however, your fire would probably go out…and your face would hurt.

Aside from this possible danger, that is it. Enjoy your flame.

Reading Maps

Authors Note: Learning to read a map is about as boring a thing to do as it is to write about, so, trust me, I feel your pain. But, as mastery of your environment is a key component to being a man, it is rather important that you understand the environment and have some idea how to get to there. This is where map reading comes in. You can skip to the next section if you have ADD.

I kid you not, the law dogs seriously want me to put in another disclaimer here. Here is what he wrote: "Please add a disclaimer about going out into the wilderness. Someone could use this book and immediately try to take on the wilderness. Something about baby steps should be included, working up from navigating in areas where it would be hard to get lost or easy to get help to gradually more intense environments." I am at a loss. If you were planning on picking this book off the shelf and then running off to the jungle, I think there are several other things we should talk about like "impulse control" and "horrible judgment." If you plan on using this book as your sole source of information for survival, you will die.

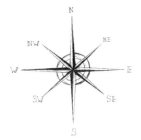

Let me ask you a few questions: Where is the closest map to you at this very moment? Seriously, do you have a map of *anything* right now? Do you even know where you could borrow one?

You will most likely grab your smartphone and pull up a mapping app.

This is not a map. It is a mapping application. I mean an actual map. The reason for knowing basic map and compass skills is because a map doesn't take batteries or need electricity. You aren't required to plug it in, and, therefore, it will work forever. Consider this: What if you are in the wilderness, and your phone runs out of juice? You are now lost because your phone has to be functioning and connected to some type of network in order to geo-locate your position. If you didn't know that, then you've never been outside of a city before. Sure, if you don't have access to a network and have some battery life left, you'll be able to still take some photos of nature or of yourself as you starve to death. There are satellite phones with GPS tracking as I write this that are $1200–$1600 without air time. If you have one of these, you should just have your butler carry you out of the woods as you casually read the rest of this book.

Prior to mapping programs, we actually had to use these *real maps*. I remember when the first GPS came out, we thought of it as little green voodoo box. It was called "the plugger" and was about the size of an old transistor radio or a large desk phone. You needed to have crypto in it, meaning it was encrypted. That was a much bigger deal then, too. It also took huge, weird, circular batteries. No one trusted the GPS because it was something so radical at the time, so we always relied on maps to navigate and used the GPS as a backup.

A map is nothing more than a graphic representation of the earth. A basic method of marking the earth is by lines of latitude and longitude. Latitudes are the lines that go up and down (north and south). Longitude lines go left and right (east and west). Some maps are called "topographical maps"; they have little squiggly brown lines on them representing altitude. The closer the squiggly lines, the steeper the grade; meaning if there are more and closer lines, you are going to be walking up a big, steep hill or are looking at a cliff.

Up or Down

One of the most boring subjects to teach or learn is called "intervisibility studies." The purpose of doing this is that you are able to visualize the profile of the terrain features on a map and have a reasonably good idea of what you could actually see if you were standing at that place on the map without going there, hence the name intervisibility study.

To do this, we used to take graph paper, a pencil, and a topographical map, draw a straight line running perpendicular to the contour lines, and then put a tick on the graph paper going up and down in relationship to each one of these small brown squiggly lines. Each one of these brown contour lines reflects a set number of meters or feet of height; this number is written on the bottom of the map. When you were finished, there would be a cross-section of the terrain features. The utility of that is you would reduce the amount of places you would go to on the battlefield in order to see if you could observe any given area, reducing the amount of time in enemy territory. This is opposed to wandering around aimlessly from spot to spot until you found an area suitable for the job. That means a greater chance of success of your mission. The problem was, you had to do this incredibly meticulous and boring study. I am going to spare you the lesson: If you want to learn how to do it, call me.

As a kid growing up, I never used a map because I knew the location of everything in my small world. I never saw a topographical map until I joined the service, and even then I didn't see one until I went to be a SEAL because I worked in the regular Navy where we used charts. For me, I had to learn map reading and navigation as a young guy in BUD/S. To start, we used to go to a desert environment in Jamul, California. The area was flat and open, but it had very pronounced terrain features in the distance such as distinct hills and mesas, which—for those of you that don't know—are tabletop-shaped pieces of earth that can extend as high as a couple hundred feet upward. In this environment, you could actually set the map out in front of you, look at those contour lines, and then a kilometer away from you see the real feature. It is amazing how much this practice increases your understanding of the environment around you.

If you're going to learn how to really use a map or read a map, you need to go in an environment, just like Jamul, that's really open. Do not go off into the woods because you can't see what the hills look like and all that, so I would encourage you to go to a flat spot.

How Far Have I Gone?

Let's say you're out in the open desert with your topographical map in front of you, and you see a bunch of circles and squiggly lines, and you can clearly identify the terrain features, and then the lights go out. I don't mean they actually turn the lights off on the desert, so this means the sun goes down. Or you are in what is called "closed terrain," and you can't see the hills in the distance to begin with, so you can't judge how far you have to go or have gone. To measure distance old school, you are first going to have to do some prep work. Mark off one hundred meters on the ground, then walk that distance and count your steps. A meter is just a wee bit longer than a yard. For instance, when I take seventy-one steps, I have walked one hundred meters. Then it goes back to the ancient time-speed-distance navigation equation, but *without the time*, meaning when I walk seventy-one paces in a direction on a compass bearing, I know that I have progressed one hundred meters in that direction and should be able to plot that on the map. If I have to go one thousand meters, then I'll repeat this cycle ten times. Do not try to count more than the total one hundred meters because I guarantee you will forget the number and start the road down to a cannibal incident. After you have moved for some time, hopefully near where the terrain changes, stop and see if you can identify your surroundings. If not, you mark yourself where you think you are on the map anyway and proceed. Once you practice and get this method down, you will be very accurate.

If you were a SEAL, you would go through this process without equipment and then with equipment. Then you would walk up a gentle grade, also known as a hill, first without gear, then with your equipment, and again, with the same process for walking down a grade. Once you'd done this, you would remember what your number of paces was for each variation. As I mentioned, for me, traveling one hundred meters is usually seventy-one paces on flat land with no equipment and eighty-two paces when going up a hill with all of my equipment because more steps are needed. This is easy to visualize if you have ever walked up a hill in your life, or walked up stairs for that matter. Your steps are closer together to compensate for the increased workload. Keep in mind that the number of paces you count depends on the terrain you are traversing, and you may have to throw in a good guesstimate if you are moving up and down hills.

Compass Skills - Marking Direction

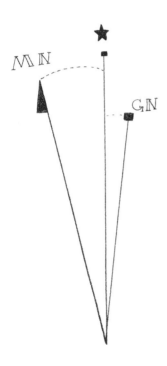

There are two different ways to note direction on a map: One is magnetic north and the other one is true north. There's a third called grid north, but normally it and true north are pretty close together, you will still need to check the difference if you plan on using this marking system. Please note that your compass is *not* actually pointing to Santa Claus's house, but a little to the west and south, meaning somewhere in Canada. Now, true north goes right into Santa Claus's living room because it is the top of the world and right on the center of the North Pole. Grid north is used for MGRS: Military Grid Reference System. The entire planet has been mapped by the military, and these grid lines are lined up, generally speaking, almost completely to true north again. In other words, maybe the guys with the aluminum hats and bunkers in their yards are on to something.

If you look on the bottom of the map where there is a bunch of writing, there's going to be a little pointer thing and there should be a star on it. That's going to be true north. So look at your map, and then on the bottom next to that, there would be one with an arrow on it. That's magnetic north. The difference between those two is going to change depending on where you are in the world. The farther away or the greater an angle from magnetic north, the greater the distance between true and magnetic north. That number is expressed in degrees and called "declination." You're going to need to understand the declination of where you are working if you want to use true north.

Let's take a second and talk about the compass. There are two different types: the model we use predominantly in the SEAL teams is called a Silva Ranger, and that's just like a regular old compass without any fancy bells or whistles on it. The other type of compass that's used mostly by the Army when they're doing artillery is called a "lensatic compass." In this model, you've got to flip up two little things and mark it in millimeters instead of degrees and…let's just say it's confusing, so we're not even going to talk about it.

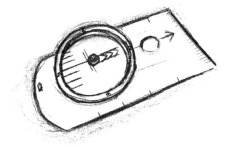

You will notice the compass is divided into 360 degrees like a circle. North is on the top and south is on the bottom until you turn the bezel, and then it moves around. The "needle" will continue to point north. There are also scales on either side of the compass. They are for measuring distance on different scales of the map, so, for example, 1 to 25,000 or 1 to 50,000. The smaller the second number, the greater the detail of the map. It is easy to remember if you think that, the small the number, the smaller the things are you can see on the map. Again, this number is on the map itself. If you want to measure distance, that will be marked out in meters or yards. That is why it is right on the compass as a quick reference for navigation.

Again, "declination" is the difference between magnetic north and true north. For instance, if you were using a magnetic compass and you want it to point to true north, if there were twenty degrees' difference, then you would have to move the compass bezel in the back twenty degrees. When you flip the compass over, there should be a small screw in there that you would turn left or right, depending on which one you had to do. Add or subtract the degrees. The acronym for that is LARS, or Left Add, Right Subtract. That means that the number is positive if you are moving east and negative if you are moving west.

This is about the time when teaching this that everyone starts staring at their shoes or resting their heads on their hands, thinking that the instructor does not notice that they are falling asleep. So, get up and take a break. For instance, I am going to get a cup of coffee. I might go to the bathroom. Why don't you bust out ten push-ups? Okay, I am back; next break I am going outside to shoot. That is the advantage of writing this on the farm.

Getting Where You Want to Go

Hopefully, you can identify where you are on the map by laying the compass at your location, lining up the little lines in the center of the bezel with the lines on the map, and then turning the bezel to where you want to go. This will give you the compass bearing that you have to follow in order to get to your destination.

From an Unknown Position

For the life of me, I can't figure out why you, a civilian, would start your expedition without knowing where you are, unless you are at a bachelor party and your friends dropped you off in the middle of nowhere with a map and compass. If that is the case, I encourage you to marry your intended, and then move as far away from those "friends" as possible because they are dicks. If you want to figure out where you are to begin with, or you want to check your present location, you do something called a "resection." If we're standing back in our desert field, maybe there's a big mountain that's directly in front of us that we can clearly identify, and there's another one that's at least 90 degrees away from us. The way to measure an angle is to look straight ahead and raise your arms out from your sides. Where your hands are pointing is 90 degrees from your eyeballs. And, of course, the back of your head is 180 degrees from the front of your head. If you find these two things that you can identify, shoot a compass bearing towards them. This means you point the compass directly at the object, and then spin it around until the red arrow, which generally points north, lines up with the other two lines inside of the compass bezel. Once the red arrow lines up in between the other lines, you read the direction or the number that's on top of the compass, and that tells you the bearing to that object. Then, you read the direction or the number that's on top of the compass, and that tells you the bearing to that object.

Once you have your bearing, look at the bottom side of your compass and what is located 180 degrees away. That's called the "reciprocal," so you measure the bearing to two different objects, then use the reciprocal and draw a line. Where those two lines intersect is where you are. That is called a "compass resection." This is made much easier if you are on a linear terrain feature like a road.

When you fly at night with a parachute, you have to navigate with either a GPS or a compass, and you have to always remember which way the compass is facing. For instance, if you were trying to fly directly north, that means you would be traveling at 360 or 000 degrees, so everything should be pointing at 360 because you're flying in that direction.

Mistakes will be made when navigating, and some will be bigger than others. Some will also take place at higher altitudes than others, and this can definitely be dangerous.

If, for instance, you are a guy I knew—we will call him John in this example of bad navigating—you find yourself making a critical error way up in the air. A bit on Military Free Fall parachuting first. There are two different types of parachuting that we do in the SEAL Teams. One is called HAHO (High Altitude, High Opening) and the other is called HALO (High Altitude, Low Opening). On this occasion, John was doing a HAHO, so, once he exited the aircraft, he pulled his ripcord open fairly quickly, which left him very high above the earth. I should probably mention that you need supplemental oxygen for this type of parachuting so you are able to fly for a very long distance through the air without a plane. You're not really flying; it's kind of a Buzz Lightyear thing, falling with style. Anyway, John opened his parachute safely and was flying through the air but looked at the wrong side of his compass. This high-altitude error caused him to fly the reciprocal of the bearing he was supposed to be going towards. In other words, he was going in the exact opposite direction than the rest of his team.

So why is this a bad thing? Well, because it is a much better idea to jump into combat joined by all your armed friends than to land completely out on your own. And, it is never a super idea to fly so far away from the rest of your team that you are out of radio range. Granted, this occurred during a training mission, but you can understand how this might lead to a little ribbing later on. In this situation, it would be very important that John understand how to do a resection in order to get back to where he needed to be. Or have a phone, or, land in a town and catch a cab, or just be able to walk a very far distance. John decided to walk.

I have learned through the years that, no matter how much time you put into teaching some people, they just can't get it right. Understanding the special relationships of the earth around you is not a skill that everybody has, and it's not a skill that everyone can learn. We've had difficulties with this in the past where guys are incapable of navigating on foot because they simply don't understand the concept of a map or even a GPS. Forget referencing a map, some even found it nearly impossible to describe the environment around them at any given time in a way that was even remotely useful.

When I was in BUD/S, there was a guy who we will call Luke who wasn't really an outdoors type. He was raised in the inner city, so he wasn't real good at map and compass. On a trip to one of the National Forests in California, we had practice compass courses that we had to do in order to graduate. Luke had his map and his compass and his PRC-77 radio which is, by the way, the same radio that everyone used in Vietnam, and he started going from one compass point to the next to the next. When you reached a compass point, you checked in with your radio for accountability. Well, eventually Luke stopped checking in on his radio.

Luke was either lost or dead. Around dusk, one of the BUD/S instructors jumped on an ATV and drove way out until he finally got Luke on the radio. When I say that people often times do not conceptually understand their place on the earth and how things relate to each other, a prime example of this shortcoming would be using an aircraft flying over you as a point of reference in describing your location to others who have sent a search party out looking for you. When the BUD/S instructor finally got him on the radio, he asked Luke if he could see a plane that was flying overhead. He was doing this to see if he was close to Luke's location. If the instructor was on a different side of a large terrain feature, Luke would be able to *hear* but not *see* the plane.

"Yes, I can see a plane," Luke said. "Okay, it is directly over me right......*NOW!*"

I think all of you can see the complete uselessness of this information. Luke then gave even more helpful information by telling the instructor he could see a woman on a horse in the distance. You can't make this stuff up. Again, if the other party trying to locate you can't see the woman on a horse because they are several kilometers away, it is not helpful. The point is that it makes no sense to use visual references that someone else is not familiar with or can't see themselves. What the instructor needed to hear from Luke was, "I'm standing next to a road," and then a description of it. The reason is that the airplane is not reflected on a map. The woman on a horse is not reflected on a map. However, the road, also called a "linear terrain feature," is on a map, and you can use it to actually find where you are on the earth.

Maps of the Sea - Charts

If you're out in the middle of nowhere and on land, you should have a map. If you're going to be navigating on the water far enough away from the coast where you can't see it, or even if you are going to be navigating towards the coast and you want to get to some place specifically, you should have a chart. To be clear, there's a map for the land and a chart for the water.

Navigating on the water is just like navigating in the desert. The Arabs used something called a "Kamal." It's an ancient celestial navigation device that tells you the degrees that the stars are above the horizon and also informs you of your latitude. I learned how to make and use one of these in a school I attended. It was swell.

Navigating on the water is very similar to navigating in the desert, as there are no discernable terrain features when you get away from the shore. To do this, we used to use a plotting board for our primary method of navigation. This board was used by the professional mariners. It's essentially a square piece of plastic with a circular piece of see-through plastic that's stuck on there with a little pivot thing and a whole bunch of lines on it. We would stick the chart for the area we were going to be operating in underneath the circular portion with the lines, and then do the time-speed-distance calculation I referred to earlier. This is the same method the ancient navigators used, and this, my friends, was in the '90s. This is how we navigated our rubber boats.

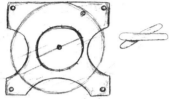 By time-speed-distance calculation, I mean we had to estimate how fast we were going, then how far we would go at that speed, and then mark it on the chart along a certain compass bearing. If you have never ridden in a small, open rubber boat in the Atlantic during the winter, this activity can be ridiculously challenging as you are constantly bouncing in the air and being hit by water. In order to measure speed accurately prior to going out, we would take tongue depressors, which look like big Popsicle sticks, and make marks on them for how far you would go if you were traveling six knots, eight knots, twelve knots, and fifteen knots. And if we were really banging away, traveling fast, we would mark a tongue depressor for twenty knots. As you are going along, you would guess your speed, and then track yourself along this chart, which is exactly what the Phoenicians used to do. For those of you who are wondering, the Phoenicians came from about where Lebanon is now on the Mediterranean Sea.

Anyway, things seemed to be fine, and then this GPS devil machine came out and things started to change. But, as I mentioned, we never quite trusted it. The communications guy would have the GPS, and he would carry that thing around like it were gold. Those old things had something called a "figure of merit" that would tell you how close, how accurate it is, and it was reflected by a number of stars on this little window. If you had five stars, it meant that you were within fifty meters or one hundred meters of where you were supposed to be, which was phenomenal back then. It is impressive how far technology has advanced today that you can push a button on your smart phone and it will tell you what seat you are sitting at in a restaurant. Back in the 1990s, fifty or one hundred meters was considered magical.

There is nothing radically different about navigating on the ocean versus the land, so don't be intimidated. Grab your tongue depressors and roll.

Maps and Manhood

Listen, I will admit that some of the processes of navigation can be challenging to comprehend. If you can't read a compass or use a compass to help read a map, it's not necessarily a negative reflection on your manhood, but, at the same time, there is a basic component about it that is. One of the most important things about manhood is to actually understand where you are in relationship to the face of the earth. Are you in Arizona? Where are you in Arizona? Or are you in New Mexico? Even though they seem very much alike, they are not the same location.

Possessing map and compass skills goes a great deal deeper than knowing your way around a fold-able sheet of paper and a piece of plastic equipment with a red arrow on it. When you start understanding where you are in the world, you understand your place. You can understand if you don't like your place in the world. If you're in a place that you don't like, you have to first identify that, and then you move on. You may not know where you're going to go; you just know you don't want to be where you are. Look for another destination. Use that map to help navigate. The analogy for that is, just as in life, that map shows you the physical surroundings, and that transcends actual forest and hills and trees and roads and buildings. It's a metaphor for your life: If you are standing in a place you don't want to be, you're going to have to figure out where you want to go. Once you have figured out where you want to go, then you have to use the tools available to you to get there. That's part of being a man.

You are taking ownership of your own destiny, and people have been doing that since time immemorial. To carry that analogy even further, two of the most important skills you can have as a man are observation and identification of truth. As you see things, as you observe them, those are the things that you know to be true. When you are consciously trying to observe things, it makes you slow down. How many times have you driven home and didn't know how you got there? You walk in and don't even see your kids in the house. You go in to a business meeting. You don't see anybody when you're sitting in a room with eight people because you're not paying attention. When you slow down, you stop looking at things and start seeing things. You start perceiving them, meaning you really understand your location.

Rural Housing Options

This book is intentionally not a survival guide. However, there are a couple of things contained within these pages that can help you out in a pinch. They are also in here because they are cool things to know how to do. I am sure this will cause a stink, but part of being a man is knowing how to do cool things. Striving to this end is also why more young men than women are killed in accidents every year. I would venture to say that they are often killed in an "accident" trying to impress a girl in the first place.

Digging a Snow Cave

If you find yourself in a frigid environment for any prolonged period of time, you will eventually need to seek shelter of some kind. There are two ways to construct natural shelters: building an igloo or a snow cave. A third way to get shelter is to remember to bring a tent. And the fourth is not to be there to begin with by understanding how to read a map.

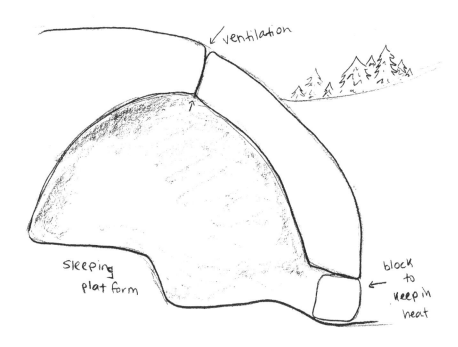

In order to build a snow cave, first you need some type of shovel. They make snow shovels, not the kind you scrape along the sidewalk in the Midwest, but they are very light, small, collapsible shovels which work perfectly for this construction because they are made for it. Next, try to find an area on the leeward side of a terrain feature. "Leeward" means it's the opposite side of the way the wind is blowing. If you take a moment to survey your surroundings, you'll notice that the wind predominantly comes from one direction. The way you can tell is that there will be more snow on one side than the other, and the character of the snow can be different because the way the wind is blowing. The snow will be thinner and crustier on the windward side and softer and more abundant on the leeward. You may have to build your snow cave here, but it is not ideal as you will be facing into "the weather."

Once you have located the leeward side where you will have the least exposure to the weather, you need to find the right spot to dig your snow cave, preferably near something that provides a little bit of cover. In a perfect world, the snow will be crusty here also, but not as crusty as the windward side. Be acutely aware of what's above you, because if you dig a snow cave in an area where there is looser snow on top, you may actually cause an avalanche, or one may happen later and bury you alive, which would be bad.

Next, take your shovel and start digging. Dig in and down a little bit, being very careful that you don't collapse the cave in on yourself. Once you have penetrated into the snow a bit, dig upwards to make a platform and a living area. Ideally, you'll have at least one other person along with you, so that if the snow cave that you're digging collapses, they can help you dig out. And if you don't have anyone there to immediately scrape and pull you out of an unfortunate and possibly fatal predicament, curl yourself up into a ball and create a space to breathe. Hopefully, your buddy will come get you before you run out of oxygen, or you are really good at being cold and not eating for days.

Your cave needs to be a little larger than you are and large enough for your equipment and another person if you are not alone. This way, you can move around a little bit without hitting the sides or the roof. Once the cave is carved out, leave your equipment outside for the time being and retrieve a candle from your bag. The candle is very important. Light the candle inside the snow cave and it will gradually raise the temperature above thirty-two degrees. Wait as the temperature increases to the point where a layer of melted snow will form, then blow the candle out, and exit the cave for a little while. This will allow the walls of your cave to become as hard as a rock and have the ability to support the snow around it. A snow cave can be built in just about any type of snow, except for really powdery snow.

Building an Igloo: The Original Man Cave

Another type of shelter that you can build in an arctic environment is an igloo. Why in the world would you ever build an igloo? If you're in a survival scenario and you don't have much food, you should try to use the least amount of calories possible. The preferred method in these conditions is to make an igloo versus a snow cave. Although it does take less energy to build, it does take a little bit more time. On top of that, it is just cool. I think every kid who is aware of snow has wanted to build an igloo at one time or another. I know I did.

For this, you will need a snow saw, which is very similar to a regular saw but with larger teeth. This tool is used for what you'd imagine…sawing snow. Snowshoes are always great to have. If you are in a non-survival scenario, you should have beer or some type of rum with you because it's more of an experience. If you have a generator, you can make margaritas, but if you have a generator you're probably not going to make an igloo to begin with.

First, identify a flat area at the minimum fifteen feet by fifteen feet in size, preferably twenty by twenty, and try to visualize a rectangle. Put your snowshoes on and walk with your feet next to each other, in the rectangle, packing the snow down as you go. Work your way to the inside of the rectangle, and then walk out of the rectangle after you've compressed the snow. The preferred snow type is the real crystalline, nice, powdery stuff so it packs down nicely. If you are in an area where the snow pack is firm enough without the stomping, you may be able to cut the snow immediately.

At this point, get a drink so you can sit down and enjoy yourself as the snow starts to harden. You've packed the snow crystals together, and they will hold the form that they have. After about a half an hour or so, finish your drink, maybe have another one. It's up to you. Then, walk into your field that you've created, and start sawing bricks out of the snow. Cut them about the size of a cinder block.

That's about 16" X 8" X 8". You can also make them bigger and thinner if you are so inclined. Once you have your field of bricks or cinder blocks made of snow, you can stack them up so they look really cool. Then find another location, preferably next to your little field, and stomp out a circle. You may be able to use the location you "mined" your snow from. Everybody knows what an igloo looks like, right? So stomp out a circle, maybe about ten feet in diameter, by starting on the outside and laying a ring of these snow cinder blocks around the perimeter. Then, before you start the next layer, take your snow saw and shave the bottom of the cinder blocks at an angle. You are going to form a spiral with this cut that will become progressively steeper in angle as you place more rows of blocks on top of each other. This snow is also perfect for making snow cones with, so you can save it for later. Or, you can put it in your margarita now.

After you lay the second row and subsequent rows, mind the angle of the blocks so your igloo does not collapse. You keep doing this and you'll notice as these layers of snow, with the angle being cut deeper and deeper, start getting closer and closer together in the shape of—an igloo.

When you get to the top, you should be standing in the middle of a little dome. The only element remaining is the cap, which is a piece of snow you take from the field that you've mashed down. Be sure to cut the cap a little bit thinner, maybe four inches, and then use it to cover the hole in the middle of your dome. Place it to cover the remaining hole.

Now you're stuck inside a completed igloo.

A lot of people have starved to death inside this part of the igloo, and it's tragic, since you have your snow saw with you, and you're sitting inside the dome made of snow.

The next step is to cut a doorway out of the wall. Make it a bit bigger than you are so you don't hit the sides or top when you crawl out. Once you are out of your igloo, make yourself a little entryway by stacking the snow bricks the same way you did for the dome.

Re-enter the igloo at this point, and follow the same steps as are found in the construction of a snow cave. Light a candle inside the igloo and allow it to get above thirty-two degrees. Then put the candle out and let the snow refreeze again. Once they harden, the walls of your igloo will be strong enough to allow you to stand on top of it. I'm not kidding. They get that rigid. Make sure to fill in any remaining cracks with snow.

You can actually cook inside your igloo if you'd like—although I don't recommend doing it for too long because, again, *it may melt; it is snow.*

Lastly, I would also like to add that, once you build an igloo, you seriously feel like a man. There is a tremendous sense of satisfaction when you are able to stand next to a magnificent shelter you have constructed with your hands. The sensation of completing an igloo is one of those things like trying to explain to somebody what it's like to have a child. You can talk about it all day long; until you actually do it, you really don't know what you're talking about.

Out of the Cold - Rabbit Holes

Rabbit holes are the ghetto of all shelters. They're easy to make, but awful to live in.

Let's say you're out in the wilderness in a high Sierra kind of area with sagebrush and such, and you are in need of shelter. What you need to do is find yourself the densest large bush in the area; if it has thorns it is even better because it will keep the animals out. To begin, you cut the branches of the bush, starting at the ground level. Continue to cut the bush until you have an entryway, then expand the hole as you get far enough into the bush to make a living space. I think everybody who has made a fort as a kid knows what I'm talking about. If you ever see a SEAL and he is at a plant nursery, he's more than likely there buying a pair of rose shears. High-quality rose shears are an essential part of your equipment when you are going out to do special reconnaissance missions.

Now, one time we had to make a series of rabbit holes on a training mission in America, and we were supposed to observe some sensitive sites. Unfortunately, the only cover available was bushes that were interlaced with poison oak. It was a five-day special reconnaissance mission, so we had to dig holes and burrow out to make these poison oak bushes into rabbit holes. They were about three or four feet tall, and we lived inside poison oak for a week. It was absolutely horrible. I don't know if you have ever been exposed to poison oak before, but at a really high level, the strangest things start to happen to your body. Your eyes swell shut, and you can't breathe very well. But probably the oddest thing I noticed was that your scrotum swells to immense proportions. I can just see a bunch of dudes running out to look for poison oak right now...

Let's talk about this for a minute.

During this training mission, we had to MEDEVAC two guys out of the field because they could no longer breathe. We were concerned that they were going to die because of the exposure to this poison oak. My lieutenant, on the other hand, decided to tough it out. Being the medic, I did everything I possibly could for him. I gave him Benadryl and an Albuterol inhaler for asthma-like symptoms. I also gave him corticosteroids, which I carried in the field, not anabolic like "you get all burly" steroids, but they help with inflammation in your throat. Still, the lieutenant could hardly breathe. At this point, his scrotum was, I kid you not, the size of a cantaloupe. I had never seen anything like it before.

"Hey man, we have to get you out of here," I said.

"No, I'm going to stay with the guys," he insisted.

"You're in charge and you get to make the decision, but I'm telling you right now, you are now a burden," I continued. "You can't walk by yourself because you can't see anything. You're a mess."

No matter what I said, he refused to be evacuated from the field because he thought that was showing leadership. He had a misunderstanding of what leadership actually means. When you're leading people, you need to be adding value and benefit to them and taking them somewhere you want to go collectively. If you are slowing people down, or in this case actually retarding the movement, then you are no longer leading.

We were still able to complete our mission, but I was not happy with the lieutenant. After we were extracted, we were able to clean up and shower on the base, and then we drove to Balboa Naval Hospital to get treatment for our weeping sores. The training guys started out ahead of us with our LT. When I got to the emergency room, we discovered they outfitted him with something called a "Bellevue bridge," which is essentially a towel that runs between your thighs. You sit with your legs spread open with your ball sack on this towel, and it prevents it from sticking to your legs. It's a medical thing; look it up. Anyway, here's this lieutenant sitting behind a little curtain, spread eagle, ball sack huge as a cantaloupe, and his eyes swollen nearly shut.

That's when I spotted two ensigns, who happened to be young girls in their early twenties. An ensign is the lowest pay grade of an officer in the Navy, also called second lieutenant in the Army or Air Force.

"Excuse me," I said to the two cute girls, approaching them. "Could I ask you something?"

"Sure," one of them answered.

After walking them over to the outside of the lieutenant's location, I whipped the curtain back. "Have you ever seen anything like this?" I asked. They gasped in horror as they saw the LT in all of his glory. I'm sure they never wanted to have anything to do with a man ever again.

Anyway, the lesson learned: Take the advice of your corpsman.

Being a guy, you should identify what needs to get done, and then go do it. On that trip, we realized once we got on location that the only place we could possibly live for five days in order to accomplish a mission—which means not being seen by anybody—was to live inside this poison oak. We all knew that it was going to wreck us. As a matter of fact, the mission took a toll because we couldn't work for two weeks afterward. It was difficult, but we had a task that needed to be accomplished, and, because we said we were going to do it, we did it. If more people actually did what they said they were going to do, I'd think we'd be a lot better off.

50 Shades of Green - Basic Knot Tying

There's a saying in the Navy: "If you can't tie a knot, you tie a lot." This pretty much says it all about those males who don't understand basic technique, so they wing it and wind up wasting materials and time. If rope, or "line" as it is referred to in the Navy, is involved and you have no idea what you are doing, you will end up with a complete mess.

So why is it important to understand how to tie a good knot?

I know you have seen "that guy" before walking along the shoulder of the highway, the one scrambling to recover all of his family's personal belongings strewn across the grass and dirt for a quarter mile. The poor goon is gathering everything with the intention of retying it to his vehicle's roof once again and hoping next time it won't unravel. But it will. He thinks that if he simply uses *more* weak knots, the problem will be solved.

Author's Note: It is important to understand that there is more to securing materials to the top of your car than tying the right knot. You also need to run a couple of lines over the materials, preferably crossed over or they will fly off no matter how good the knot. "That guy" not only loses his belongings off of the roof of his vehicle due to a weak knot, but he also doesn't use enough line to cover what he is attempting to keep secure. I only mention this because I was driving to my farm recently and spotted "him" driving on the highway with a mattress on top of his car. He had tied what appeared to be a fairly good knot in a line that was strung exactly half way across a mattress. The front half of the thing was bend ninety degrees, pointing straight up in the air. It was awesome. Unfortunately, the mattress blew off shortly after I saw this. I say "unfortunately," because, if it had stayed on there a little bit longer, I would have taken a picture and put it in this book.

Why Knot?

Knots have been and will always be important, no matter how advanced the world becomes. One of the first things we learn as children is how to tie our shoes, which, interestingly enough, the older we get, the further away we go from that to the point where we finally have Velcro straps. Don't listen to the naysayers—you can still be a man with Velcro straps on your shoes. You just have to earn them. And for people who are boating, you have to be able to tie a boat up, or it's going to drift away. There's no other way around it. You can't sit there and hold the boat until you are ready to go out on the water, right?

How many times have you actually been in a position where you know you're going to have to tie something— maybe a tarp over some items, a sign in between two posts, etc.—And you have sat there and realized *you have no idea what you're going to do?* To make matters worse, you've got an audience eagerly awaiting your performance. The only thing you want is for everyone watching to walk away so you can have a few minutes to figure it all out. You get those uncomfortable beads of sweat on the top of your forehead, your face turns red, and then you screw it up. What's even worse is when another person walks up, clearly acknowledges that you have no idea what you are doing, and then ties the knot themselves. And if you say this hasn't happened to you before, then you are lying. So let's make sure this scenario never happens again.

Isaiah Maring is a fellow retired SEAL and has been a friend of mine for a long time. Isaiah was on our jump team, which is a parachute demonstration team that jumps into stadiums and many other locations to help advertise the SEALs, explosive ordinance disposal (EOD) guys, and, I think, divers. Being a part of the parachute demonstration team is a strange gig. It gets you out of a platoon for a couple of years, you can relax a little bit, and then it's still a very high performance activity because you're doing fairly dangerous maneuvers "under canopy," as it is referred to. After getting out of the Navy, Isaiah and I briefly worked together until he moved on to focus solely on his parachuting company. I couldn't think of a better guy than Isaiah to explain the real importance of knots, being able to tie them, untie them, or to discover them where they don't belong.

You Get What You Pay For

By Isaiah Maring

There is a saying in parachuting that "packing is for poor people" because if you have the money, you can hire someone to pack your parachute for you. At one point, I had a guy, we will call him "Jimmy," packing my parachute who was making about five dollars per pack job. This may not seem like a lot, but it only takes about five or six minutes to repack the rig, so they can finish quite a few per day.

I was practicing some jumps one day and, as I deployed my parachute, I looked up and discovered there were tension knots above my head. My slider was also stuck, known as a "hung slider," which means the slider is above the tension knots and not allowed to come down. The slider is a piece of material that helps slow down the opening of the parachute at terminal velocity so it doesn't snap open in a quick second, but actually takes about four to five seconds instead so you have an easier opening.

If the slider does not come down, it will not allow the canopy to fully inflate and make a "flat wing," therefore increasing your descent rate quite fast. As if the hung slider wasn't enough, tension knots also appeared, which shortened the lines on one side of the canopy. When this happens, it can put you into a right- or left-handed spin very quickly. Fortunately, I immediately saw the problem, reached up to the opposite set of lines and pulled them down evenly so it leveled the canopy out, so I had a little bit of time to figure out the situation.

I then looked at my altimeter and saw that I was about two thousand feet, fifteen hundred feet being the lowest that I would be able to "cut away" and pull my reserve. I was in San Diego over some hills, so fifteen hundred feet was based on the drop zone, the lowest area where I was going to land, and I was a little bit over the hills, so I probably had even less space. Cutting away means getting rid of the bad canopy and the bad lines above my head.

The typical procedure to get the knots out would be reaching up as high as you can, pulling them down as low as you can, and then letting them go. In doing this, hopefully the force of the line slacking and then going taut again will pull out the tension knots and allow the rope to come free. I pulled on it about ten times and nothing came out. I gave it one last shot. I pulled it down to my waist, let the line slack back up to go taut, and it came out with I was roughly fifteen hundred feet, so I was able to come in and land on the main canopy without having to cut away.

As I was pulling down on these lines, I thought to myself that five dollars was not worth somebody else packing my rig if I had to cut it away and have a potential loss of a main canopy, which costs a couple of grand, as well as an eight-five dollar reserve repack for a rigger to pack it.

Lesson learned: You get what you pay for.

Square Knot

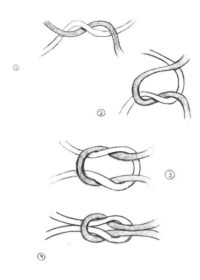

We're going to start simply. Let's say you're going to tie something to the top of your car, but you realize you don't have enough of the original material to begin with, so you have to connect one piece of line to the next piece of line. You're going to tie a Square Knot. It's the easiest, simplest thing. Take the two ends of the line, which is called a "bitter end," and place one side over the top of the other. Then simply fold them over each other so the pattern goes, right over left, left over right. Or, left over right, right over left. Pull that together, and that's a Square Knot. You want to leave about an inch or two on either side of it so that it won't slip out under tension. Done.

Bowline Knot

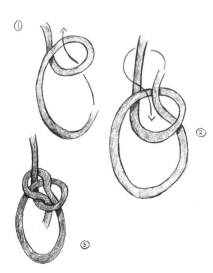

Why would you us a Bowline? When you want a circle of rope that will not come undone. If you need a field-expedient Hangman's Noose, this is a great way to do that. Actually, I can't imagine any circumstance where you'd have to do that. I mean, I think if you're going to hang somebody, you should really put a lot of thought into it; if you're going to put that much thought into hanging someone, preferably, in the grand scheme of things, you should probably be involved with some type of criminal justice system, so it's not something you're cooking up in your basement. And then if you're going to be that serious about your job—which, if you're a true man, you should take your job very seriously—then you should actually learn to tie a Hangman's Noose. Some things are important enough to learn how to do properly.

You've probably heard of this knot before: It's the one where you have the rabbit, the hole, and then a tree. Anyway, take the bitter end (again that's the very end of the line; the other side in technical terms is called a "running end") and lay it on top of itself so you make a circle. If you're right-handed you should be holding the circle in your left hand. Then, take the bitter end—this is where the hole in the rabbit tree comes from—and pass it through the back of the hole that you've just made, around the tree, then back around through the hole, and pull it tight.

And you've got a Bowline.

There's one big loop on the back that runs towards what you called the tree. If you take this knot, and put it under a tremendous amount of tension, you can break that little loop. It's called "breaking the back" of the knot, and it will come untied regularly. This will allow you to retie it later on if you want, or it can just be an open-ended piece of line.

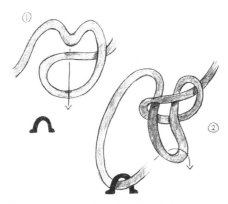

Trucker's Hitch

Okay, back to the guy on the side of the road. He may have tied a Trucker's Hitch as the knot appeared to hold even as the mattress flew into traffic. I will say, and don't take this the wrong way fellas, I try not to take a lot of life lessons from truckers. This is kind of general as a rule to live by. It just seems like that's not the well that you want to go dip a cup of wisdom out of. Now, granted, I think the trucking industry has improved greatly since the advent of mandatory drug testing, but, for a while there, probably in the '70s and 80s, you definitely didn't want to pick up advice from truckers.

Anyway, a Trucker's Hitch is designed to secure items and materials in a manner so that the knot doesn't come untied until you want it to. There are two components of a Trucker's Hitch: an Overhand Knot and a Half Hitch.

So, the first thing you want to do is make sure you have enough line to secure your particular item or items. Let's say you've got a canoe, because men canoe. I actually do not like canoing at all. Anyway, so you have enough line to secure whatever you want to secure to the top of the car, and then you tie an Overhand Knot.

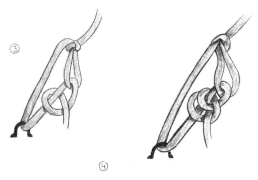

Make a little loop in the line, and then pass it around itself in its entirety, and pull it through. You now have a knot that will not come untied later. This is not like the Bowline or the Square Knot because it will not come untied once it's under tension. Then, pass the running end of the line around your item, and you'll wind up passing it through the loop that you just made. Then you pull it tight until you secure your cargo. Next, you're going to pinch the running end of the line right next to the loop, which almost resembles a Square Knot. You make another small loop with the running end, pass that end through, and tie in a Half Hitch that will hold that in place. You do two or three of those, and it looks very cool. That's it.

That, I should mention, is a simple, one-stage Trucker's Hitch. You can repeat that, the initial Overhand Knot, further down the running end of the line if you want to get your cargo really secure.

Wrap Up

There are so many more skills to learn if you are going to spend any appreciable time outdoors somewhere other than Central Park in New York City. What is important is that you get out there and have a look around. Getting out of the house and unplugging makes you slow down and appreciate things you never will if you are watching them on television. You may think you are experiencing things, but you are actually just watching someone else experiencing something. You are hearing a story, but you are not part of it.

CHAPTER IV

Hunting-Gathering

There is a famous quote by Ernest Hemingway who was a big game hunter and also served in the Spanish Civil War as an ambulance driver. He said, "There is no hunting like the hunting of man." Hemingway was referring, of course, to warfare and his participation in these events.

Basic Hunting Strategies

Basic hunting strategies really are the same in almost any environment. For starters, make sure the animal that you're hunting actually can be found in the environment. Next, check with all of the local officials, and educate yourself on the laws and regulations. Lastly, select the right type of ammunition. There's an old joke, but it's true: In prehistoric times, what did they call a vegetarian? A bad hunter.

If you are going to go hunting, it is very important not to be drunk. It doesn't matter what you may be hunting. You should set off on your expedition sober and remain this way until your day is over. Unfortunately, this is a basic safety tip that a lot of people violate, but this is plain common sense.

Hunters, farmers, and fishermen are the best keepers of our environment, so be smart and understand that an awful practice that should never be a part of your hunting strategy is poaching. Folks up in the rural areas who do a lot of hunting don't make a ton of money, but they certainly know the environment and understand what is detrimental to it. Support your local community by finding a local guide and learning what animals are in season.

The remaining tip in terms of basic hunting strategy is *don't shoot yourself* because, if you ever do, you will ask yourself two quick, panicked questions. One, did anybody see me shoot myself? And two, will I die if I don't go to the doctor?

They are very important questions that, hopefully, you'll never have to ask yourself.

You may have noticed that animals are much more aware of their surroundings than human beings, and that's generally because they don't have access to the Internet. I firmly believe that if the animal kingdom ever gets the Internet, they'll be much easier to hunt because they're just going to sit around on their asses and watch television and probably surf porn, like human beings. Then you will just be able to walk up behind them and hit them over the head with a bat. But until that happens, we need to learn a little bit about the animal kingdom.

For one thing, they are acutely aware of what's taking place around them, particularly when it comes to what they smell. If you were going to hunt a deer, you would position yourself downwind, meaning, if the wind is blowing from west to east, you want to be on the east end of the field if you expect the deer to come from the west. Those critters can smell things from a long distance, and they will just avoid you completely. Since the human odor is so strong, in order to counteract it, they sell deer pee. Seriously, I'm not kidding—pee of deer. Its purpose is not only to cover up your scent but doe urine also attracts male bucks. This is also a big difference between deer and humans; I don't know what *you* are into, but this is not my thing.

The second sense of animals to be concerned about is their hearing. When you're hunting, you have to be *very* quiet, or, if you decide to move, also position yourself downwind. Only move when other things move around you naturally to cover your sound, meaning, when the wind blows and rustles leaves, it's easier for you to move and not be detected because the sounds that your feet make as you're walking are covered by the sounds of the leaves blowing.

The third sense needing mentioning about animals that's more pronounced than in humans is sight. While some animals can see in color, others are color blind. Deer are allegedly color blind, so when you are hunting them you can wear clothing that is camouflaged in nature, but is actually orange. This is very important because, as I mentioned earlier, some irresponsible people are drinking heavily as they're hunting with firearms. The bright orange color may prevent you from being shot.

Camouflage

Personal concealment is not only essential in battle but also when hunting. Camouflage comes from the word, well...*camouflage* I believe, and its main purpose is to mask your form and hide you from your prey. There are no right angles in nature, so if you look at a fence post, that is a perfect right angle. They don't really exist naturally. The closest forms I can think of are branches on a pine tree when they grow directly perpendicular to the trunk. Other than that, those V's that you have in your shoulders and in between your legs when you're standing are not typically found in nature.

The key to camouflage is breaking up the pattern of the human body with either color schemes involving brown, green, red, gray, or tan, depending on your environment, or different hues so that your body outline no longer appears to be a human. This can also be done with objects. For example, although it needs to be replaced frequently, natural vegetation is outstanding and makes it very difficult for you to be seen as a person in the field. When I say "in the field," I don't mean actually in an open field. It is an expression used by military people to mean somewhere outside of your base in the wilderness, which could be anywhere.

Another principal of camouflage is you attempt to match the environment that you're in. We're going to remove the right angles and match the environment, meaning the color schemes surrounding us. Let's say, for instance, you're walking on the Serengeti Plain, where you have tall, brown grass, but then the trees are green. You could wear desert tan pants with a green woodland top, so the casual observer would have difficulty spotting you among the trees and the grass.

Another successful way to use camouflage is to hide inside something. A little structure such as this is actually called a "hide," or if you're hunting for birds, it's called a "blind." I don't really know why it is called a blind; it doesn't blind the birds, and you can obviously still see. If you're hunting land animals, you're going to hide in a *hide*, but if you're hunting fowl, you hide in a *blind*. Which begs the question, if you were hunting a penguin, a flightless bird, would you hide in a blind? I'm not sure I know the answer to that one.

When you are stalking an animal, it is best to keep solid objects between the two of you in order not to be seen. That's called "dead space," meaning, if there's a tree, for instance, you can't see through the tree, and whatever is on the other side cannot see you. So you can approach the target directly by using this dead space. That is an effective technique for stalking.

Let's tie these all together: sight, sound, smell.

During a training mission back in Virginia, a friend of mine and I split off from the rest of the platoon as a pair when we were conducting a special reconnaissance mission. We were trying to find the headquarters of an American artillery unit that was unaware we were there in the area. When we eventually narrowed to the area where the unit was located, we left our equipment in a cache site as we set off into the woods.

Our first step was to cover ourselves in fresh natural vegetation, making sure to break up the right angles I discussed earlier. At that point, we decided to stalk as close to the unit as possible using dead space downwind from where we thought the headquarters was located. When we finally located the headquarters tent, we intended to sneak up and take pictures of the maps that were posted on the wall inside. I followed as my friend moved in closer until he came to a log. We were both crawling, but it was too low for him to get under, so he got to his feet, cradled his rifle so the barrel was right in front of his face and the butt stock was near his crotch, and stepped over the log. And then, as he was in mid-squat, someone walked straight out of the command tent directly towards us. I was still lying down about four feet behind him, and we both thought that we were busted, which would have been incredibly embarrassing.

However, instead of confronting us, he stopped about six feet from me, turned around and dug a cathole with his heel of his boot. By "cathole," I mean he scraped a hole with the heel of his boot about three inches deep, and then dropped his pants and started going to the bathroom. We remained completely still, as my friend was squatting over the top of a log holding a rifle and I was lying on the ground while the Army guy was squatting over his cathole. The professional enlisted man in me was very bothered by this as a cathole should be at least six inches deep. I decided not to comment on his lack of field craft due to the circumstance. Needless to say, it was a very stressful moment for the two of us. When this unknowing soldier was done with his business, he pulled up his pants and walked back into the tent. That's when my friend looked at me and made a danger signal or a cut signal— you may know it as making a knife-hand and making a motion like you're cutting your neck. At that point, we very gradually moved out of the area.

Now, what did we learn from that? One, we were stupid for trying to get that close to something to gain information that wasn't worth it. Two, camouflage works.

Hunting Small Animals

Many people, including SEALs, do not know how to prepare small animals to eat. The reason is that, in the majority of cases, it is wholly impractical to hunt, clean, and cook animals on a combat mission. This is true with the exception of conducting a long-term mission with host nation personnel that require an extended stay in the local environment, or "going indig," meaning folding yourself into the culture in an unconventional warfare type scenario.

Many people have found my ability to eat just about anything remarkable. I think that it is a function of being raised without a lot of money. I do not recall *any* lactose intolerant, gluten-free, vegetarian-foodie-complainer-pants in Luverne, Minnesota. You either ate the food that was there or you did not eat. None of us died.

Snakes

To answer the first question that probably entered your mind: Yes, snakes taste like chicken—really tough, rubbery chicken. I've eaten snakes in the Philippines, the United States, and in Malaysia where I ate a large Boa.

In my mind the best method to kill a snake is to pick up a stick, put it on the snake's head, and then take out your knife and saw the head off. I know this is not very dramatic, but it is quick and effective. I'm not sure if you are aware of this fact or not, but snakes continue to move for a short period of time after you've killed them. So does just about everything else.

The best way to clean a snake is first to get a sharp knife. If the snake you intend on consuming is venomous, you have to cut past the poison glands, which are right behind the head. Keep in mind that if you don't cut far enough back, at least a couple inches behind the skull, and remove the poison glands, you will wind up poisoning yourself—which may sound kind of funny, but, let's be honest, it would be an incredibly awful mistake on your part. Next, lay the snake out with what used to be its head away from you. If you want to stretch the skin to dry it, this is the method you should choose. Stick the point of your knife into the snake's butthole, also known as the "anus," making sure not to stab yourself, and run it all the way up to where its head used to be. I personally do not like the term "anus"; I don't really know why.

If you're not concerned with keeping the skin, make a quick cut and pull the snake apart like you're taking a sock off your foot, turning the snake skin inside out. Either way, following the skinning, you need to stick your thumb inside of the carcass, pull the guts out, and a scrape your thumbnail along the spine. That, my friends, is it. You can wash it off if you want, but you don't have to, and stick it in the fire. You can wrap it up in banana leaves or something like that, or you can drive a stick through like a skewer, cook it until you feel comfortable eating it, then dig in. It's actually not bad.

Squirrels

It's very important that you select the right type of bullet for what you're hunting and your skill level. If you're a beginner hunter that is not a great marksman and hunting for squirrel, you probably want to use a 20-gauge shotgun instead of a .22 rifle. As we talked about in the weapons section, a shotgun shell contains a bunch of little BBs that will make it a bit easier to hit the squirrel. The down side of using a shotgun is that several of the BBs may hit the squirrel and damage the meat. There is not that much on the critter to begin with. If you are a good shot, you can transition to a .22 rifle and aim for the head of the animal to preserve as much for dinner as possible. Don't use this technique if you plan on mounting the squirrel head. There is no way you fell for that.

In Virginia Beach there was a twenty-five-meter range on the base for the SEAL Teams to use for sighting in our weapons. It was right next to the ocean with a high berm to prevent the bullets from zipping out into the ocean. On this particular day, I was in a platoon, and we were just about finished sighting in our guns. If you remember, sighting in an M4 at one thousand inches replicates the distance of your three-hundred-meter "battle sight zero."

Just as we were about to have another course of fire, a squirrel ran out on top of the berm in front of the sixteen of us SEALs on the firing line. The guy running the range was our Command Master Chief, a southern guy with a heavy southern drawl.

"Nobody better shoot that damn squirrel!" He yelled out. And then after a pause, he said, "Ready on the left. Ready on the right. All ready on the firing line. Fire at will." And with that, all sixteen of us shot the squirrel at exactly the same time. I can't say I was all that surprised when it just kind of went *poof* and essentially flashed into this little plume of gray smoke.

Now this is a perfect example of the type of weapon and ammunition *not* to use when hunting for squirrels. This is also a perfect example of how SEALs can read each other's minds. No one smiled, looked sideways, or winked at each other. We all just *knew* that we were *all* going to shoot the squirrel.

Just so you are aware, this is the overly complicated method of doing this. You can just cut the squirrel open in your hand and roll.

Once you have hunted one properly, take the little fella, flip him upside down and put his head down with his rear feet up. Take nails and drive one through each of his rear feet into a tree in order to hold the carcass firmly in place. Just as when you started to cut the snake, find the squirrel's butthole. This is a point of reference. You're not sticking the knife in the squirrel's bunger you're going to be tenting the skin *near* there. That means pulling up the skin a little bit so it forms a little tent. Stick the tip of your knife into the squirrel, and make a small incision. Cut around the back of the anus. Then continue that incision all the way up (in reality, down because the carcass is inverted) his belly and up his front legs, forming a "V." Repeat this on the hind legs. Once you have done this, start to peel the fur back by pulling the tail down.

You will immediately have to cut through vertebrae of the tail to continue peeling the fur off. Do this very carefully or you will cut through the fur itself and not have a complete skin.

Once the fur is peeled down to the neck of the carcass, you are going to have to cut around the back of the head to remove the fur.

Once you get the fur off the animal, stick your knife in the anus, trying not to get so far into the guts that you spill the contents of the bowel inside of the abdominal cavity. Put your fingers inside, pull out the guts, scrape the stuff away, wash everything off, and then you are ready to cook.

Squirrels taste like dark turkey meat, for you information, and they're excellent. First, add a little bit of salt and pepper, then cook over an open flame for about fifteen minutes.

Bats

Not long after Joseph killed the "baam-boo viper" with a simple step of his flip-flop back when I was attending Jungle Environmental Survival Training (JEST) in the Philippines, we finished our insertion patrol and settled into our base camp. After getting ourselves squared away, it was time for some jungle food gathering. Joseph walked us to a stand of green bamboo and showed us that some had very small slits around two centimeters long by just a couple millimeters wide. He explained that if you took your bolo, which is a big machete made out of the leaf spring from a truck, and hacked into it right above the little crack, you could pry it open and look for bamboo bats inside. If, in fact, you do find a bat, you close it back up and cut above and below that section of bamboo. It holds them in this little container. You can then wrap it up with some leaves and throw in the fire to steam the bats. As the bat is steaming, you make a skewer out of another piece of bamboo. After a couple of minutes, the bats are removed from the original bamboo, and then you run the skewer through them from shoulder to shoulder, lining them up next to each other. It's a bat-kabob.

As we were cooking our bamboo bats in the fire, I asked Joseph, "So, what do these bamboo bats taste like?"

Without pausing, he looked back at me with a serious expression. "Uh, they taste just like the big bats," he answered. That is one of the coolest things about traveling the world to areas where tourists generally do not venture. You get to experience cultures as they actually *are*, not how the people who live there *think* you would like to experience it.

Joseph was operating under the assumption that everyone around the world regularly consumes fruit bats and that I would understand the reference.

On a strange note, since the departure of the US military from a permanent presence in the P.I., JEST is now a tourist destination. You can find it on the Internet.

Frogs

Being a frogman myself, I've always been uncomfortable eating frog legs, but, then again, being hungry makes it a lot easier.

Oddly enough in the country of Vietnam where SEALs first got their fierce reputation from, they serve a great deal of frog legs. I know this because I encountered it when I participated in a Joint Task Force—Full Accounting (JTFFA) mission there. JTF-FA is a completely unclassified mission that focuses on attempting to recover human remains from American Missing In Action (MIA) service members. I participated as a medic. The mission is divided into two separate but complementary groups or small elements. The "Investigative Element" (IE) involves traveling around the country interviewing folks to find out where crash sites were for airplanes and helicopters or anywhere it is suspected that there may be remains. Once you have done your investigation, then you go out to see if there are any artifacts at the locations. If there is sufficient evidence to suspect the presence of human remains, the site is recommended for excavation. In comes the "Research Element" (RE). This group comes in and sets up archaeological digs just like you would see in National Geographic. Overall, I think the mission allowed us to heal some wounds left over from the war, both on the Vietnamese side and the American side.

The first month, I spent my time driving around as a member of an IE, and the second month, I spent on an RE.

We drove from Da Nang, an airfield that had served as a big Marine base during the Vietnam War, all the way to Hanoi and then lived on the Cambodian border.

During these travels, I noticed every time we stopped they had frog legs on the menu. Finally, I decided to order them and found out that, just like a few other small animals, they tasted like chicken.

In order to prepare frog legs, first, you have to catch the frog. Normally, you do that with something called a "frog gig." It looks surprisingly like the Trident on a SEAL Naval Special Warfare device. It is basically a big fork with barbs on it attached to a pole. When you spear these little fellows, try to aim for the body or the head; try not to hit the legs because there's not that much meat on a frog, believe it or not. After you spear it, make sure it is dead by whacking it on the head with a rock or another object.

Now all that is left to do is skin your frog.

Take your knife, stick it in the belly, and make an incision through the skin. Try not to cut into the stomach, otherwise the guts are going to come out and make a mess. Make a small incision, run it down the leg, and then just peel back the skin. This is much easier with a pair of pliers. It is really that simple. You can cut the legs off first and then skin them, but I prefer to use the body as a "handle" to hold while peeling the skin off. Finish everything off by baking, frying, or barbecuing over an open fire. Add a little salt and pepper—the Vietnamese sprinkle MSG on it, and some soy sauce.

Basic Fishing Strategies

For those of you who have never been fishing, I feel sorry for you. It is an ancient activity that really allows you to connect with your environment. It is an activity that can be relaxing, exciting, rewarding, but also endlessly frustrating. It is kind of like golfing in a boat.

When I was attending Survival Evasion Resistance and Escape (SERE) training, they talked about having Escape and Evasion (E&E) kits. In the SEAL Teams, we were actually provided with these. The composition of these kits varies, but there is always a little fishing hook with some fishing line, sometimes a lead sinker. Now, I have thousands of dollars' worth of fishing equipment—rods, poles, reels, lures, bobbers, you name it—and fishing is still a challenge. So, let me do you a favor and tell you what to do if you come across the hook and line in one of these kits—go ahead and get the fishhook and just gouge your eyes out with it. That way you won't be able to see how miserable you are, because unless you're in some incredibly abundant waters, you're not going to catch anything. You might as well ask the fish to surrender.

When you're fishing, you're generally either using live bait or some type of simulated bait. You could also be using a net, but I doubt it. Personally, I believe live bait is more fun, not because you're skewering some little animal with a piece of metal, but because it seems to be more productive. If you're going to fish with live bait, you're going to have to figure out some way to get the bait on the hook. For those of you who are a little squeamish, this can be viewed as gross, because, really, in the end, all you're doing is impaling a small creature on a huge piece of metal.

The two most common types of live bait are worms, which I am certain everyone is familiar with, and minnows. If you're capable of talking a worm or a minnow into hooking itself, then you don't have to worry about the rest of this, but the chances of that are very unlikely. A minnow is a small freshwater or saltwater fish, and they range in size and species; I would say the typical minnow is maybe an inch or two long. A night crawler is a very large worm, relatively speaking to other worms. For some reason or another, a lot of them come from Canada. I don't know what they have going on up there, but you will often see Canadian night crawlers. They're called night crawlers because they come out at night. I have no idea if they like maple syrup.

Worms

How do you hunt for worms? The best way I have found is either to wait until it rains or take your garden hose, wet down your lawn, and let it soak for about fifteen to twenty minutes. If you do this in California, they will hunt you down and throw you in jail for using the water. Then go out at night with your flashlight, and the worms will have come to the surface. You have to be very careful when hunting the worms. Of course, they can't see the flashlight because they don't have eyes, but they can certainly sense the ground moving. As soon as you grab the worm, it's going to try to get back into its hole. Oftentimes they break, so you have to develop a feel for how much pressure to use so you don't damage your bait.

Grab the worm and regard it. You will notice there are two ends: the head end and the tail end. You can figure out which one is which. There's a band that's about two-thirds of the way on one side of the worm or the other; the short side of the worm is the head end. Also, you can tell the head end because the skin is a darker color and pointy. The backside of the worm is more flat and a lighter shade.

Next, take the hook in your hand and squeeze the worm a little bit to get its attention. Then take the hook, push it right on the tip of what would be the head end, and slowly feed the worm onto the hook as you push it through. Make sure the barb of the hook comes out of the worm at some location. Now, you can leave stuff hanging off the end or try to get the whole worm on the hook, but it's important that you get the barb through the skin; otherwise, the worm can actually get off the hook, which would just be a travesty.

Minnows

Big fish eat little fish, so in understanding this you realize the importance of little fish in fishing. You can trap minnows, or you can buy them. Personally, I have never trapped a minnow, but I have bought plenty.

There are a couple different ways to hook a minnow. One is you take the hook and run it perpendicularly underneath the dorsal fin—that's the fin on the back.

The second way is to hook the minnow from underneath its jaw through the top and in between its nostrils. Yes, fish have nostrils. Now, you may say this is cruel, and I guess it could be, but if you go around and look at young people today—and this makes me sound like a curmudgeon—but a lot of people have more metal shoved in their face than a fish or worm will ever have, ever. And remember they did that voluntarily.

Once you have your hook baited, you will need a location to fish. You probably should have done this first. If you did not, I can just imagine you sitting in your living room with a minnow on your hook getting progressively angrier. Your best chance of catching a fish is to understand what the bottom of the body of water you intend on fishing looks like. The reason is fish like to hang around weeds, logs, and holes. As you're looking at the water, if you can see a fallen tree in the water, I would suggest casting near it. Unfortunately, the areas where fish like to gather, weeds and underground obstacles, are also where you're probably going to wind up catching your hook, meaning you can snag it and end up losing your bait and your rig. This can become frustrating, just like golf. It's the equivalent to losing your ball.

Growing up poor in the Midwest, I often used to go fishing for bullhead, which are small catfish essentially. I'd catch them at the gravel pit for our family reunions and fill up five-gallon buckets. Gravel pits are just places where certain types of small rocks are in abundance. A mining company comes in, starts digging out the rocks in an "open pit" operation, and keeps on digging until they hit groundwater. Once they do, it fills up with water, and then fish magically appear. I really have no idea how they get in there to begin with, but there always seems to be fish in them.

When I was at SEAL Team FOUR, we used to be geographically assigned to South and Central America, just as the Seventh Special Forces Group (Airborne) or 7th SFG (A). Those are US Army Green Berets. Whenever we traveled to these regions, I always brought my fishing poles along, so they started calling me *El Pescadero*, which means The Fisherman. I appreciated the name because it was a way to get to know the locals and their culture. When you're fishing, it doesn't matter if you speak the language or not. You're participating in the same activity and have the same ultimate goal.

A long time ago, the United States and Venezuela maintained good relations, so we used to work together. I have no idea if that still happens today. On a training trip, we spent a month driving an LCU, which is a Landing Craft Utility, down to Orinoco River. An LCU is a boat similar to the Higgins boats or MK 6 boats and MK 8 used in the film *Saving Private Ryan*, just way bigger. During our time in Venezuela, we taught Venezuelan marines how to do river and stream crossing and counter-narcotic operations. My responsibility as a corpsman was to make sure that I had a full understanding of the environment, meaning dangerous plants and animals in particular. If something happened, I needed to have the ability to medically treat everyone properly.

One of the first questions I asked was whether or not there were piranhas in the river because we were expecting to be doing river and stream crossing and spending a lot of time in the water. My Venezuelan counterparts assured me that there were no piranhas, and I took them at their word as they would be with us in the water.

About two weeks into our trip, I decided to take a little time to fish off the back of the boat. Unfortunately, I wasn't having much luck. I would get a bite, pull my line to reel in the fish and feel the line break. I replaced my hook a few times, but this kept happening. Finally, I decided to attach a steel leader to the end of the fishing line. A leader is a very thin cable that reinforces the line where it comes in contact with the fish. Once I attached this, I again cast my line out and hooked something. I quickly reeled it into the boat and lifted my catch out of the water. On the line was a four-inch fish with a red belly and *huge* teeth.

I turned to the Venezuelans. "Hey, man. I thought you told me that there is no piranha in this river," I said.

One of them responded, "There are no piranhas in the river. That's a caribe."

"A caribe?" I repeated.

"Si, it's a *cousin* of the piranha."

I learned a couple lessons that day. One, ask very specific questions when the issue involves whether there is a chance you could have your nether regions eaten by fish in a river in Venezuela, or anywhere for that matter. And two, more importantly, I found out that the caribe, a smaller cousin to the piranha, are excellent when cleaned properly and served with a little bit of lime.

Fish

I asked Mike Higgins to explain how to clean a fish for very specific reasons, the first one being he owns a company called The Fish Guys in Minneapolis, Minnesota. Mike imports from around the world and knows more about fish, types of fish, and how to cook fish, than any person I know, which is interesting because I only recently met him on a plane. We sat down next to each other and started talking, as fellow passengers do sometimes. Eventually, the topic of our conversation moved to what we do for a living. What really piqued my interest about Mike was that he took a company that was not doing well, and, through a lot of hard work and ingenuity, he turned it around and made it productive and profitable. To hear him talk about the people that work for him is like listening to a guy talk about his family. It's abundantly clear that Mike cares about the men and women immensely. Quite frankly, this is a huge portion of being a man: seeking out responsibility and then being responsible.

I was very impressed with him after even a short conversation, and he reminded me of a bunch of guys that I grew up with. It seemed like we had known each other for years. I couldn't think of a better guy to explain how to clean fish properly.

Cleaning Fish

By Mike Higgins

CEO The Fish Guys

THE
FISH GUYS

Mike Higgins is an entrepreneur who began his career trading commodities at the Chicago Board of Trade in the early 1990s. He loved the fast-paced environment of the busy floor but realized he wanted to trade something more tangible. He wanted to be able to feel closer to the commodity he worked with each day. Mike exchanged grain for seafood when he purchased Minneapolis-based The Fish Guys, Inc. 2005. He was able to marry his dual interests of commodity trading and fishing into a career and was successful in turning a distressed business into a prosperous one. The Fish Guys now sell more than eight million pounds of fish and seafood each year. Mike and his wife, Jenny, love to cook together with the help of their three boys. Together, they also love to fish, entertain, and eat well...so the career change suited the family well. The boys enjoy fishing the many waters Minnesota offers year-round.

5320 W. 23rd Street
St. Louis Park, MN 55416
www.thefishguysinc.com

Since fish are a gift from God, they are owed a tremendous amount of respect. I built The Fish Guys on the virtue of respect for the sea. In fact, our company motto is, "Respect at Every Step." This is something I try to teach to my boys as well.

Sixty percent of the seafood I sell is fresh, and the vast majority of that is hand-cut. Filleting a fish by hand is much more efficient than using machines...and more respectful. This method not only results in a fresher product, but it is also the best way we can utilize more of the amazing fish. In order for a fish to be machine cut, the fish first needs to have had rigor mortis set in. This means more time that the fish is not ready for consumption. Hand-cut fish, on the other hand, represent freshness, care, and respect. When a fish is recently cut from the bone, it naturally tastes better. It may cost a bit more, but, in my opinion, this is a non-negotiable means to the end.

Filleting a fish properly is all about the knife. You absolutely must have a flexible, sharp, sensitive knife that is appropriately sized for the fish you are cutting. You need to listen to that knife, and let it talk to you. When the tip of the knife hits the bone, you need to be able to hear it, feel it, and be able to act accordingly.

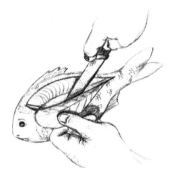

Whether you are filleting a crappie with your buddies in an ice-fishing house or cutting something as magnificent as Alaskan king salmon, it is essentially the same process. First, make an incision through the skin on the back of the fish, along the dorsal fin, running the knife from the head to the tail, along the ribcage. As soon as you feel the rib cage, the midpoint, listen to the knife and cut through the entire fish. As you work your way down the rib cage, all of a sudden you won't feel rib bones anymore. That is the underside of the fish, and you don't want to pierce its guts. Next, run the knife along the whole side of the fillet to the tail. Keep the knife pointed down, but not too far down: You want to be able to get the maximum yield—again, out of respect for the fish.

I teach my sons that a fishing trip is a lot like life. Success comes from being prepared, something I learned from my own father when we fished the Great Lakes when I was a boy. When my boys and I leave to go fishing, we try to be prepared. Not only do we need our rods and tackle boxes, the appropriate bait, and safety measures, but we also need to watch the skies and be responsibly aware of the weather ahead. Mother Nature is not to be messed with and must also be respected. Not being ready for anything is setting yourself up for failure. Be prepared. And always have a backup plan. Sometimes, even when we prepare everything correctly, we still may not catch anything. That's a life lesson, too. Other times, we might catch the big one. And there is no sweeter reward.

Basic Patrol Formations for Hunting of Man

Back to Hemingway's statement: "There is no hunting like the hunting of man." With all the crazy technology you read about on the Internet, there really is nothing like packing your stuff up with your buddies, arming yourself heavily, and then walking around looking for trouble.

- There are some very basic formations for doing this if you are in a group. The formation you choose to walk in depends on the type of terrain and what you're trying to do. It's just that simple. If, for instance, you're walking through closed terrain like a dense forest, you would more likely than not opt to walk in a file formation, which is one person in front of the other person. The advantage of this is that it is really easy to control. You know where everybody's at, either in front or behind you. You can get through tight spots and the "signature," meaning what you look like, is pretty low except for from the sides.

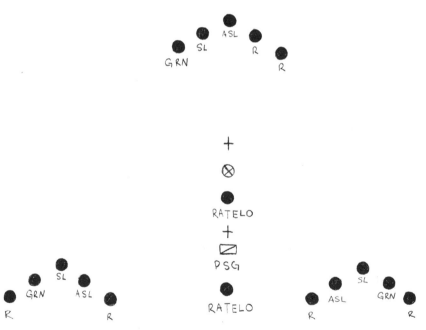

If you are in more open terrain like a desert or a field, or even a sparsely wooded patch of ground, you may want to opt for something like a wedge, which resembles an inverted V. This formation gets you spread out so you have nice dispersion between the folks so you don't all get whacked if someone drops a mortar round on you. It also puts more firepower forward if you are anticipating running into an enemy.

Another type of formation is called "on line" and, no kidding, you are basically on a line shoulder-to-shoulder with the guys you are walking with. You should be spread out a little bit farther than that, maybe two to four arm's lengths in between, and then walk forward. This is generally used when you want to have most of your firepower going forward, and you know where the enemy is located.

Tip: It's also an excellent way to find your car keys if you drop them in a field.

There are several other types of formations that you can use depending on what goal you are trying to reach, whether or not the enemy is out there, whether or not you know the enemy is out there, the amount of people, and the terrain. An excellent reference for this is FM; it stands for Field Manual 3-21.8. It used to be known as FM 7-8. The Infantry Rifle Platoon and Squad.

Hunting and gathering skills are just that: They are skills. Hundreds of books and magazines have been written about this subject, but there is no substitute for finding an Old Timer to go hunting with. Harvesting animals must be done in a sustainable, responsible manner. Follow the local laws and regulations to make sure that your children and the future generations can enjoy Creation.

I started this chapter with a quote from Ernest Hemingway: "There is no hunting like the hunting of man." It recently dawned on me that maybe he was thinking about himself when he made this statement. You may or may not know that Ernest Hemingway committed suicide by shooting himself in the head with a shotgun.

I feel compelled to share a note on suicide as it is taking a toll on my military brothers and sisters. So let me say this, if you think there is no hope, I am telling you there is. If you think no one cares about or loves you, you are mistaken. If you think things will never get better, they will. I am telling you this from personal experience. If you are feeling like there is no light at the end of the tunnel, please call the number below. Be a man and do it. You are worth it.

National Suicide Prevention Lifeline
1 (800) 273-8255
Hours: 24 hours, 7 days a week
Languages: English, Spanish
www.suicidepreventionlifeline.org

CHAPTER V

Automotive

When my youngest son, Daniel, recently got his driver's license, I walked him over to the front door of our house and pointed outside. "Boy, do you know what you call that thing up in the driveway?" I asked him.

He looked at me quizzically. "A car?"

"No, boy, that's *freedom* right there."

Even though my son responded by nodding in agreement, I could see he didn't understand the full meaning of what I was trying to tell him. In his defense, how could he? You really can't tell someone about freedom; it is something they have to actually experience in order to understand. It wasn't until a few days later, after Daniel had driven off to see his friends and cruised around town, that he began to recognize the newfound sensation I had told him about. I could actually notice the change by the bright expression on his face. As a parent, I thought this was a great moment for two reasons: One, it is fantastic to see your progeny becoming a fine young person, and, two, I now knew I had significant leverage for any future issues that may arise. I am not above coercion when it comes to parenting; you should look into it.

That look on Danny's face must have been pretty close to the one I also had at sixteen years old after I got my hands on the keys to my first car—a 1969 Toyota Corona, not a *Corolla*, a Corona. It was red with a thick, white racing stripe running down the center and sported a four-cylinder engine that would top out at sixty-four miles an hour. Not sixty-five, but *sixty-four*.

Part of being an American is our strong sense of freedom. And what could be a more tangible expression of this than young men driving, fixing, jumping, and racing around in cars? A car provides young men with the ability to make decisions on the direction they want to travel and where they want to go. If you so choose, you can do all of these at a very high rate of speed. Mostly, I chose to.

Peter Parker, yes, *Spiderman*, knew "With great power comes great responsibility." Well, the same goes for freedom. Act irresponsibly and your parents will take your vehicle away. Act like a complete jackass and law enforcement will shut you down. You don't become a man by doing stupid things to lose your freedom, but sometimes you need to do ridiculous things in a reckless manner to understand responsibility. As a young man, you typically want to test the bounds of what you and your vehicle are capable of.

Hell on Wheels

My first car was so light that my buddies would open the passenger and rear doors and hang out of the opposite side when we were going around corners to offset the weight like we were sailing a catamaran. My friend, Eric, owned a zippy little orange Mazda GLC, and we figured out a system where, if we drove exactly twenty-five miles an hour, we could open the passenger door and dive out of his car into the thick hedges without getting injured. For some reason twenty-five miles an hour seemed perfect. Trust me, we tested it. Although we did these things out of foolishness at first, in the long run it provided us with a sense of respect for the capability of the vehicles we owned. It also went a long way to show that, in fact, young men's auto insurance should be much higher than young women's. Come to think of it, that was just stupid.

An unfortunate fact about cars is that you can only experience the amazing sensation of freedom if it actually runs. Many of us grew up having first cars that were less than fully operational; in other words, they were beaters because we did not have that much money, and our parents were smart enough not to spend much on a car if they chose to help buy one at all. Roadside assistance? No. Unless you count someone anxiously standing on the side of the road with a thumb out, hoping to get a ride to the next gas station. The best way to solve a problem is to not have the problem in the first place. Sun Tzu said this in a roundabout way. He was right.

Radiator Fluid

Radiator fluid is generally a mix of water and anti-freeze. Its purpose is to cool the engine; however, it does it in a different way than oil. Radiator fluid gets pulled inside the engine by a water pump that's attached to a fan in the front of your vehicle's engine. Please note that this is something you never want to get your fingers stuck in. The fluid circulates and then continues forward to the radiator—the big metal block with the thin ribbons of metal—yes, those things you want to take your finger and push down on, but doing this can damage your radiator, so never touch the front of it.

As you could imagine, running out of radiator fluid will cause your engine to overheat just as when you run out of oil, but muck quicker. In older cars, you have to add radiator fluid directly to the radiator by removing a silver cap and pouring it in. The cap is similar to the cap on a prescription bottle—push down and rotate to remove it.

Whenever you're checking your radiator, you have to be extremely careful of two things: 1) If it's hot, the boiling water will come flying out of the radiator and burn you horribly, and 2) again *if it's hot, the boiling water will come flying out of the radiator and burn you horribly.*

On old-fashioned cars, if you have to add radiator fluid or water to the radiator to cool it down, you want to make sure the car is running so the engine would be continuously pulling the water or anti-freeze into it in little streams, as opposed to one big gush as it would if you filled the radiator up by itself. The reason being, if the car was shut off and you filled the radiator full of cold water, when you started it, the car would pull an entire radiator's worth of cold water into a hot engine block. By doing this, there is a good chance the engine would be damaged. The dangers involved in opening the radiator cap and also not pulling too much water into the engine block at a single time have been solved in newer vehicles with the addition of an overflow or filling reservoir.

It is incredibly important to know what you are pouring where. If you look in the engine of your car, there are going to be two things that appear to take water. Of course, they'll both take anti-freeze, and they'll both take windshield wiper fluid as well. One is, in fact, specifically designed to take windshield wiper fluid, and the other one is the radiator overflow reservoir. It's pretty easy to tell one from the other because the windshield wiper fluid reservoir will have a picture of something that looks like a windshield with a wiper running on it and fluid flying out of it. Generally speaking, the cap is blue. The radiator reservoir oftentimes is black with yellow letters on it. It says something like "radiator."

Don't let this confuse you because it is not a trick.

Once again, start your car and look at the level. There should be something on the side of the reservoir that says "add" and "full." Once the car is running, go ahead and add fluid to this reservoir until it's full.

Gauges

My brother-in-law, John, owns a BMW parts reclamation outfit in San Diego, California. He is essentially the Rain Man of the BMW world. You can say, "1973, BMW 2002," and he will immediately reply with something like, "Heater motor issues, get an after market one, and don't worry about it." I was speaking to him about cars as I do sometimes and asked him about the gauges in the dashboard. I was wondering if they were accurate and needed to be checked frequently. John looked at me and said, "Derrick, they call them idiot gauges for a reason." And that was the end of that discussion. John is not a big talker but when he says something, you should listen. And with that, we are going to go with John's short but great advice: Look at the gauges frequently and don't blow them off, or you will be the one they are named after.

It makes complete sense to me to include another John in the automotive section even if it may confuse the reader. The second John here is John Rauch. John is married to my cousin, Margaret Mulligan, we know her as "Peggy" and she is one of the sweetest, smartest, and toughest women I know. She helped raise my brother and me and still helps my family every day. We love them very much. Any dude that can equal Peggy in a relationship is a real man. And—he knows cars to boot.

John Rauch

Owner of Jackson Auto

Thirty-five years ago, I answered an advertisement to sell cars, and, all of these years later, I am still fascinated with this business. The technology on the vehicles has evolved from the days when I could repair a car myself, but I still look forward every year to the new changes made to each make and model of vehicle. Take the time to take care for what you drive. That is what men do.

Oil

By me, not John

Oil. There are many kinds of oil. Engine oil is a fluid that comes from the ground. It goes through many machines, including transportation trucks and ships, before it gets to your car. Olive oil comes from a tree and goes through many machines, including transportation trucks and ships, before it winds up in your salad. Peanut and vegetable have similar journeys before they wind up in front of you. The oil we are going to talk about is the first one mentioned, engine oil. It is the byproduct of hate and the scourge of those who do not understand how an economy functions. I say this because many of the people in the region of the world who produce this magic black elixir despise America, and most of the people who demand freedom from the stranglehold of this fluid really don't understand the depth of the dependency we have on oil as a nation. I, for one, would gladly never use fossil fuels again, but I am into eating and not walking everywhere.

Internal combustion engines must have oil because it not only functions as a lubricant but also cools the engine. Depending on the make and model of the vehicle, it will require a specific viscosity and volume of oil. "Viscosity" is a fancy word for "thickness," and "volume" is a big word for "amount."

You will see oil labeled something like "10W-30" or "10W-20." Those alphanumeric codes reflect how the oil behaves in relation to heat and cold. But, as this is a practical guide, I am here to tell you that unless the container says "peanut oil" on the side, you will be okay if you stick it in your engine. The amount of oil that an engine requires depends on the size, just like the amount of food a person consumes at an all-you-can-eat Chinese buffet. You can rest assured that if a bus load of sumo wrestlers rolled into a joint they would receive significantly more scrutiny than a truckload of supermodels. This is because of volume. Most engines require anywhere from 4 to 8 liters of oil depending on the size of the engine, just as sumo wrestlers require between four and six liters of shrimp fried rice as an appetizer.

Engine oil is typically dark yellow in color before being placed in an engine. Until very recently, all motor vehicles were manufactured with a dipstick in order to be able to manually check both the level and roughly the condition of the oil in the vehicle. Newer, high-end cars are being manufactured without the ability to check your own oil in recognition that people no longer do so. Although this may seem like an advancement for motorists, in fact it means that people will have to bring their vehicles to a shop to do routine maintenance. Good for the shop and manufacturer, probably good for the car, but a reduction in choice for the owner. Having a choice equals freedom. Freedom is awesome.

Note there is a difference between oil and transmission fluid. Transmission fluid is what lubricates and cools the transmission—the box that makes the gears go. When you shift from drive to reverse to neutral, you're manipulating the transmission and the fluid aids in this movement. Transmission fluid is typically red/pink in color and can also be checked by pulling the dipstick. When you check your fluids, first make sure your vehicle is on a flat and even surface. To check the oil, the engine has to be warm, so turn it off and wait a few minutes before moving forward. In order to get an accurate reading of the vehicle's transmission fluid, be sure to keep the car running while checking the dipstick. If you do these in the reverse order, you're going to get a bad reading and possibly wind up putting too much oil or transmission fluid into your car. And you certainly don't want to do this because you will risk blowing the engine and wrecking it.

I would love to say that I learned the importance of looking at the gauges and keeping the proper amount of oil and fluids in a car by reading about it, but that is not the case. When I was stationed at Concord Naval Weapons Station in Concord, California, I borrowed a friend's old truck when he went home on leave. As I was driving, I noticed that the temperature gauge was a bit in the red; actually, it was as red as the collective eyes in Dublin the morning after St Patrick's Day. However, I ignored the gauges and pressed on. After about thirty minutes, the truck started to sputter, and then the engine shut off. I pulled the truck over and my head out of my ass to see steam and smoke pouring from the engine compartment. The engine had gotten so hot that the pistons had essentially been welded to the inside of the engine. Needless to say, that was the last time my friend lent me his vehicle.

Tires

There is nothing as pathetic as an under inflated tire, sitting soft and squished under the weight of a vehicle. It sort of reminds me of when I have eaten too much and then look at my belly hanging over the waist of my pants. It doesn't look good, and it sure doesn't "drive good," as I've heard race car drivers say. With modern tires you cannot just look at them and guess; there are steel belts that help give the tire form, and they can make the tire look like there is more air in it than there actually is. Fortunately, tires are very easy to check. How you know how much air pressure is required inside of a certain type of tire? You're in luck because it's written right on the side of it. On each tire it'll specify what the maximum operating pressure is in units called PSI (pounds per square inch). One atmosphere of pressure is 14.7 pounds per square inch. That's the pressure you experience at sea level. It is the actual weight of the air column on your head. In case you are about to run out and go scuba diving, you should know that every thirty-three feet you descend under water, you pick up another atmosphere. Wherever you are this weight is called ATA for ATmosphere Absolute.

What happens if you don't check your tires? Worst-case scenario, you crash because you lose control of the vehicle. Best-case scenario, your tires wear out faster and you have to spend more money on them. That is a crappy best case. When you check your tires regularly, you have a lower chance of having them pop. Your vehicle handles better, and you also get better gas mileage. Still, despite maintaining proper pressure in your tires, if you drive long enough, you will eventually get a flat tire. I once had two at the same time because I ran over a board with nails in it. These things just happen.

If your tire goes flat or pops, you'll be able to feel it because the steering is radically effected. As with most things in life, panicking does not help, so you should not waste any time doing it. The vehicle will more likely than not "pull" in the direction of the flat tire, meaning if the flat is on the left or driver's side of the car, that is the direction the vehicle will veer. If this happens to be towards oncoming traffic, you need to do the following steps very quickly or you will be a candidate for leading man in the next episode of *Blood on the Asphalt.*

Slow your speed by taking your foot off of the gas pedal and *not* by slamming on the brakes. If you do this, the car will move even more radically. Direct your vehicle to the side of the road or the safest direction. Once you are there, take a moment to reflect on your near-death experience and un-pucker your butthole. You are still alive, so get over it and move on. Time to change the tire.

Tires

By my older brother Kurt

Kurt Van Orden is my older brother. In high school, he worked at a gas station back in the day when many of them still had service bays for changing oil, tire repair/sales, and tune ups. When he left Oregon to attend college in Wisconsin, he actually "willed" his position at Chevron to me and then took it back for the summer following his freshman year in college when I joined the Navy.

Kurt eventually graduated from Portland State University with a degree in business administration and marketing, and today is self-employed in packaging sales. He has one daughter, who, for the record, can change a flat tire on a vehicle.

Changing a Tire

By Kurt Van Orden
Owner Empaqt Packaging

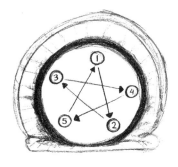

The knowledge and ability to change a flat tire on a car, much like auto insurance, is something you need but hope you never use. For the purposes of this lesson I'm going to assume that you are without roadside assistance or don't have two hours to wait for a tow truck to come and assist.

Step One: Perhaps the most important thing you can do is get safely to the shoulder of the road and apply your emergency brake. Make sure all four wheels of your vehicle are out of the lane *and* you've given yourself sufficient room to open the driver's side door to get out. This is especially important if you've pulled over on the right shoulder and have to change a tire on the driver's side. Turn on your flashers to increase visibility—it's generally the button with the triangle—and if you happen to have an emergency roadside kit that has flares this would be a good time to use them. In Europe, interestingly enough, drivers are required to carry small reflector triangles to use whenever pulling over to the side of the road. These are put at least twenty-five yards behind your vehicle.

Step Two: Locate your spare tire. At one point in time, older makes of vehicles came with a full-sized tire matching those already on the vehicle. Now, manufacturers equip cars with space-saver tires, often referred to as "donuts." They are narrow and not exactly built to last. I wouldn't recommend driving on them at more than fifty miles per hour and exceeding seventy miles in total distance.

Step Three: Once you've removed the spare tire, you'll also need your jack which uses mechanical advantage to lift the vehicle up. Position the jack under the frame of your vehicle.

Step Four: Then, take the lug wrench (or "tire iron" as it's called in some circles) and turn each lug nut about a quarter turn. ("Lugs" are just a fancy way of saying a screw that goes into a tire. A lug *nut* is a cap for this threaded bolt coming out of the drum.) You may have to jump on the tire iron to accomplish this because chances are that the person who last put on your tires used an impact gun to tighten the lug nuts. This is normal. The loosening action is referred to as "breaking the lugs." Of course, you're not breaking them, but you're merely breaking the seal. You have to do that while the tire is on the ground because as soon the tire is up in the air it's going to free spin with it. Once you have turned the lugs a quarter turn, jack up the car so that the bottom of the tire is about an inch off the ground. *Never ever jack up the car until you've turned the lug nuts while the car is on the ground.*

Step Five: Remove the lug nuts in a star pattern as shown in the illustration, and put them in a safe place so they don't get lost. Note: when you tighten them back up you will use a similar star pattern.

Step Six: Remove the flat tire and put the spare tire on the vehicle.

Step Seven: Tighten the lug nuts in a star pattern until all of them (likely five) are snug.

Step Eight: Lower the car to the ground and tighten the lug nuts the rest of way. Like before, always tighten them in a star pattern as shown in the illustration.

That's it. Wash your hands off. Smile at yourself in your rear view mirror.

You should take your vehicle to a gas station soon after changing a full-sized replacement tire because the mechanics will use a pneumatic wrench on the lugs so that they can tighten them with the proper amount of torque.

Please note that all of this information can be found in the owner's manual—yes, that thick booklet in your glove compartment that has gone relatively untouched. And contrary to popular belief, most men actually read directions. I read directions, and I ask for directions if I'm lost. There is no sense in driving around aimlessly like a goofball.

Alternate Uses for a Jack

From time to time, a jack for a vehicle can come in handy for other purposes, as I found out while driving a HMMWV (Humvee ®) Humvee during training in Northern California late one night. The key difference between driving at night as a SEAL and as a civilian is that as a civilian you generally have your lights on. We, on the other hand, do not. This is a skill that must be trained to and works best when you have night vision goggles on. If you don't have night vision goggles on and are driving at night with your lights off, you have more likely than not been sipping grandpa's cough syrup. On one particular night, we were driving in a dry riverbed and had come to a spot where the sand was so soft that we would get stuck if we continued forward. Normally, in these conditions you simply drive faster to use momentum versus traction, but, as I said, this was at night on a training mission where we were in uncertain terrain, meaning the "enemy" could be near. This is no time to barrel forward recklessly.

In trying to turn around, I backed the Humvee®—this vehicle that weighs six thousand pounds—lengthwise onto a fallen tree. I rode straight up until I lodged the thing on the frame. Even though there were four of us in the car, we couldn't move our vehicle at all. My first instinct was to call AAA to have them send a tow truck, but then I realized it would be a bit awkward explaining why we were wearing camouflage paint and had machine guns. Fortunately, we were trained by some great guys. One in particular is named Tim, who is a total gear head. He had taken the time to show us how to use the jack as a pivot to extricate a vehicle in this situation. It took us about forty-five minutes with two guys working the jack and two holding security. Even though we were in training, you still conduct yourselves as if you were in combat. We had to jack the Humvee ® up and then push it off the jack probably about fifty times because we could only move it *six inches* every time. What's the lesson learned there? Pay attention to short SEALs who train you on how to undo something stupid that you have done, and, as always, make mistakes in training so you don't make them when it counts.

Driving—From Slow to Fast

And, you guessed it. Time for and yet, another disclaimer.

Just about everything I describe in this chapter with cars is dangerous. There are several schools that teach this stuff, including with Larry at Sealed Mindset. It can be a hoot doing this stuff, but you need professionals teaching you, or a huge amount of liability and collision insurance. Huge.

The first thing I taught my children about any vehicle they would be operating—whether a motorcycle, ATV, car, or truck—was how to stop. This is because I have never crashed anything that was not moving. It is also because I know that within five minutes of driving it, they will try to see exactly how fast it will go, so there is no need wasting time with that. I know you cannot fight genetics; pushing limits is in their blood as it is in mine.

In the SEAL Teams, we are incredibly harsh critics of all things, especially of ourselves. Iron sharpens iron. This carries over into every aspect of our professional careers but manifests itself dramatically when driving. We have some of the most naturally talented and motivated people with the best training in the world, but woe be unto you if you err, especially if you are behind the wheel. I am sure that any professional race car driver would suckstart a pistol if they had to drive a group of SEALs to the grocery store. I'm telling you, Dale Earnhardt, Jr. could not drive our bus well enough. The peanut gallery of SEALs would crush his soul and leave him on the side of the road sobbing. So you can imagine that a normal driver would probably pull the bus over on the side of the road, put the transmission in park, open their door, and run. This, of course, is assuming that we did not throw him out of the window as the vehicle was still moving.

Fastest Car in the World

You know you want to know how to do it, so let's talk about high-speed driving. To be sure, anyone can drive as fast as the vehicle they are in will go, but not everyone can do this and not destroy the car and kill themselves. The Fourth Law of Thermodynamics states that: *the fastest car in the world is any rental*. So, if you want to practice driving fast and reckless I would get one of these. This is, of course, a joke. Or, is it? I would get at least two of these because if you are relying on this book to show you how to drive fast and well, you will at a minimum crash one of them.

If you want to drive super fast, it is really easy. Just stomp on the gas pedal and steer straight. If you are on a runway or the Bonneville Salt Flats in Utah, you will be fine. Where a lot of people get in trouble is when they have to *turn* the vehicle.

SEALs with Wheels

SEALs attend several driving schools where race car drivers teach us something called "apex driving." The apex of any corner is where it starts going the other way.

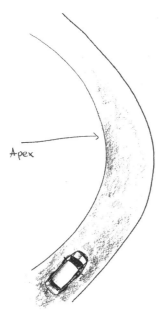

Apex

Some corners do this more than once, but for the sake of our discussion, we will stick with the single apex corner. When you look at a corner, visually pick the center of that curve, right where the most significant change in direction occurs. This is the "apex." As you are driving, what you want to do is swing your car wide enough to the right or left, depending on the curve, so that as you sink into the corner your wheels will be as close to the apex of that corner as possible. This apex point is the innermost point of a line taken through a curve. What you're doing is essentially straightening out the curve, and that's how you can maximize your speed.

Braking Bad

Most people think that driving into a corner as fast as possible is the best way to *exit* the corner as fast as possible. However, this is not true. The chances are that, if you enter a corner as fast as possible, you will exit the corner about halfway through, only seeing the end out of the back of the ambulance that is taking you to the hospital for emergency surgery. This is assuming that it is not a hearse taking your mortal remains to a cemetery where you will be taking a permanent dirt nap.

Braking Good

To decrease the chances of an untimely death and increase the chances of you hauling ass through the corner in complete control, you need to bleed off speed by doing something called "threshold braking." Threshold braking is when you apply the maximum brake pressure *without* skidding. When you do this, you'll feel that tires screech, and you let up just a little bit. When you slam on the brakes and start to skid, little balls of rubber form underneath your tires and cause you to lose traction on the road. You are essentially sliding on rubber ice. When you let up on the brake a little bit, it clears those balls out, and you are able to regain full control.

To recap, riding on tiny rubber balls can lead to death. This may be a universal truth.

The key take away from this is that once you actually enter into a curve, you should not have to apply pressure on the brakes as this can lead to you losing control of the vehicle. You should have bled off enough speed by threshold braking, so you negotiate the curve until you reach the apex, and then punch it. Again, you should only apply your brakes inside the curve if you are going to crash because by applying your brakes in the curve, you increase your chances of crashing.

Speeding without Speed

To ask why a man craves speed—meaning velocity, not meth—is to ask a question about our basic nature. Why do we, as humans, continue to explore the world around us even after we have checked off all levels of Maslow's hierarchy of needs? In short, because it is fun. Not all things need to be a profoundly transformational growth experience; sometimes doing stupid things is just entertaining. To become a man, you must explore and understand boundaries and limits, or you will never understand how things actually work. In our culture, oftentimes this is done by young males in and around vehicles. Ask yourself why a sixteen-year-old boy's car insurance is much more expensive than a sixteen-year-old girl's. There are two factors that contribute to this: 1) testosterone, and 2) testosterone. A man should strive to be the complete master of his environment, and, in order to achieve this, you truly need to take it to a level where you encounter failure.

Ideally you would do this in a methodically well-thought-out manner so that you can gain the most from the experience, but in reality, the chances of that hover around zero. SEALs routinely train to the point of failure. We do this so that we absolutely know what we can and cannot do at any given point. This is a function of professionalism. If you are choosing to push a vehicle to its limit, you need to do it in a controlled setting, preferably with professional training. Or, you can be a jackass, count on luck, and hope you live long enough to see the light. I am still waiting for the light.

Executing a J-Turn

Let's talk about some trick car moves. The driving schools SEALs attend also educate us on how to drive in any environment with almost any type of vehicle.

I believe it is incredibly important that a man should be able to operate almost any piece of machinery that he comes in contact with. I do draw the line at aircraft. I certainly wouldn't walk out to a flight line, jump out on a plane, and take off because I don't know how to fly. I think I can figure out how, but the landing part would probably be *challenging*.

Everybody has seen high-speed car chases in the movies where a car is being chased by another, and they are about to escape when they encounter a roadblock. This also happens on a regular basis in Los Angeles. Just when it appears all hope is lost, the driver slams the car into reverse, whips it around 180 degrees, and flees in the opposite direction. This is called a J-Turn. It may look spectacular and incredibly complicated, but it's actually one of the easiest trick moves you can learn in a car.

Focus, my people.

The first thing you need to ensure is that you will not kill anyone other than yourself as you practice this. This particular maneuver also works great on a gravel surface as the lack of traction will make the swinging of the vehicle easier. Just make sure it's not a gravel road with steep embankments on it. Start on a flat surface and stop your car, but leave the engine running. Put the car in reverse and start backing up; you do not need or want to go faster than twenty-five miles an hour. When you hit this speed, turn the steering wheel a quarter turn, and only a quarter turn, to the right or to the left. The vehicle is going to start spinning around. *Do not apply the brakes.*

At this point, take your foot off the gas pedal. When the front of your car gets to about ninety degrees from where you started, meaning you are now perpendicular to the road, slam the car into "drive." The car will continue to spin around until you are facing in the opposite direction from where you started. Now, stomp on the gas pedal. No kidding, it's that simple. I've executed J-turns in up-armored Humvees ®, regular Humvees ®, vans, and trucks. I have not tried it on a motorcycle for obvious reasons.

"PIT-ing" Another Vehicle

In other action sequences in movies, and especially during those live police chases you see on television, you have probably seen instances when the police are chasing somebody, and they eventually ram the car from the rear, causing it to spin out. They are not actually ramming the vehicle; they are doing something called a "PIT maneuver" or a Precision Immobilization Technique. This technique is also known as "tactical ramming," "tactical car intervention," or "fishtailing." And, above the speed of twenty-five miles an hour, the car could roll, so this can be a fatal event. Again, it's way easier than you think.

When the following car drives up behind a second vehicle, it is important to closely match the speed of that vehicle. If that vehicle is going fifty miles an hour, you want to go fifty miles an hour and get to the right or the left of the vehicle. Again, at this speed, you may cause the target vehicle to roll over and kill the occupants, so this should only be done under professional supervision. It is much easier to do on the driver's side because your line of sight is clearer. That means the driver's side of your vehicle is approaching the passenger's side of the lead vehicle.

While matching the speed closely, ease up to where the front quarter panel of your car (that's the part by your front tire) is near the rear quarter panel of the leading car. This is basically right behind their back passenger tire and right in front of your driver's tire. Still matching your speed, go up and slowly touch the front of your car into theirs, and then gently move the wheel over. You're *not* smashing into the car or jerking your steering wheel and careening into it. Done properly, you are slowly pushing the rear end of the lead vehicle so it slides out, causing the wheels to catch and the vehicle to spin around. What's interesting about the vehicle spinning, or being pitted by the one following it, is frequently it will stall.

Jumping a Vehicle

We talked about how to maintain and change your vehicle's tires in order for them to operate properly while on the road. I think it is important to acknowledge that there are times when tires actually leave the ground.

While I was in Iraq, we often drove around in up-armored vehicles. This means a vehicle that appears to be a normal car, but it is, for lack of a better term "bulletproof." I say this because, in the end, nothing is really bulletproof. An up-armored Chevy Suburban is a very heavy vehicle, and by itself weighs about 9,500 pounds. On one particular afternoon, I was in the last vehicle in our convoy following a Suburban that was loaded full of rockets and machine guns. In the event that we got into real trouble, this vehicle would be able to provide us with extra firepower. As I followed the Suburban, we noticed a suspicious car coming from the opposite direction on the road. By the path it was traveling, it looked like it was going to pull into our motorcade. It wasn't uncommon for vehicles to cross over into our lane, mostly because they did not realize we were traveling in a convoy. In these situations you don't have the time or ability to have a conversation with the other people; you just have to assume they are acting with malicious intent.

The guy driving the lead vehicle, the Suburban, suddenly stomped on the gas and headed in the direction where this car was going to cross over into our lane. Fortunately or unfortunately, there happened to be a pile of compacted dirt that was about a foot and a half high in his path, and, in order to block the vehicle, he hit this pile traveling probably sixty or seventy miles an hour. When the Suburban launched, it created a huge cloud of dust that briefly blinded our vehicle. Luckily for us, we were still able to catch a glimpse as this vehicle weighing 9,500 pounds and full of rockets, machine guns, three Team guys, hand grenades, other explosives, and cutting tools soared through the air.

I must say that it was phenomenal. After the mission, we returned to our safe area. The driver got out of the suburban and was quick to apologize.

"Chief, I am so sorry..." He told me.

"Stop. Just stop it," I said. "That was the coolest thing I've ever seen in my life."

Not only had he landed the Suburban safely and did not crash, but more importantly, he blocked the other car from coming into our motorcade. That was the driver's first responsibility, and he acted flawlessly.

This is a solid example of how—once you understand the capabilities of the vehicle, and you practice, practice, practice—you can perform what appear to be near miracles. You should be the master of all equipment and of your environment to the best of your ability at all times. Knowledge about a vehicle's capability is similar to what we say about carrying a gun: It is better to have it and not need it, than to need it and not have it. However, if you have it and don't know how to use it, well, then you are just a male.

Glamorous life of a SEAL Corpsman *"Burning the S*@#ers in Panama"*

In The Jungle, 1995

Force on force training in the jungles of Panama.

Graduating from BUD/S

On the Mountain in South America where I Figured Out SEALs did not know
how to start a fire

Bosnian house

With former President, George W. Bush

Bosnian church

Machine gun training as a new guy

About to jump in 18D

Reenlisting with one of the best Skippers I ever served under.

Hanging out in Jajce, BiH. Same town Tito fought the Nazis from.

Humvee training in the desert

Dive training in the pool

Hoist Training. This is about three hours before
the same helo crew almost killed me

Machine gun training as a new guy

Winning the hearts and minds by distilling booze in Bosnia

My last deployment to Afghanistan. The guy next to me was and is one of the greatest officers in the SEAL Teams

Free-fall parachuting

Fishing with my oldest son and late father-in-law, Dr. Tom Whitelock

Prior to speaking at the Marine Corps Ball in Estonia

Graduating from BUD/S

I just got done jump mastering a "Duck" in Virginia.

Real men curl

CHAPTER VI

First Aid

First aid is just that—aiding someone first. Even if you have a phone and can call 911 in the US or 112 in most European countries, the person in question very well may bleed to death in front of you if you do not take action. Learning advanced medical techniques takes years, and they even have a school for this. But learning how to keep someone alive for a relatively short time until help arrives is really not that difficult. For some reason or another, I have had many experiences with medical situations, even before I became a corpsman and a SEAL. And I am glad to say that all of them turned out well for me. I am still here writing this. Many of the people I treated died, but I guess that is why they call it medical "practice."

The first person I can remember saving was a young boy around ten years old. I was working at a movie theater in Oregon when a lady came out dragging her son by the arm. He was nearly blue. She was screaming and generally acting up, saying her son was dying. I just grabbed him, spun him around, and performed the Heimlich maneuver on him. At that point, an Everlasting Gobstopper—a round, hard candy—popped out of his mouth and into a metal ashtray, and then I let him go. The mother grabbed him and stormed out of the theater without so much as a "thank you." I really hope that kid turned out to be a pain in the ass as a teenager. What is the moral of this story? See a problem; fix the problem. Don't freak out.

Learning medicine takes time to learn the basics. Hopefully, this chapter will help a bit, but I encourage you to take some formal classes. Your local community college is a great place to start.

First Aid

Mark Donald is a physician's assistant, which means he's a healer, and he was SEAL, which means he's a warrior. Mark has been one of my best friends for well over twenty years. In fact, he was my mentor going into the SEAL Teams and showed me what it meant to be a true professional. Mark is an incredibly unique individual, lives his life with high-energy, and is a short, unstoppable force. As if that is not enough, he also happens to be the recipient of the Navy Cross, the Silver Star, and the Bronze Star for valor. I could not think of anyone more qualified than he to discuss first aid.

First Aid

By Mark Donald

Partner JIC Global

Mark Donald is a partner at JIC Global. A service disabled veteran company that utilizes medical and scientific competencies to solve complex military, civic, and international health mission sets.

www.battlereadymedic.com

Every Marine prides himself on a few things. The most obvious is being a Marine, but not far from the top is their ability to sharpen and hone their knives, most importantly the KA-BAR. The K-Bar to a Jar Head—and *being one myself* I speak the term with affection—is the equivalent to the katana of the samurai. Elegant weapons can awe and inflict damage upon one's enemy, yet somehow still be viewed, as a piece of historic art requiring reverence among warriors. PFC Esteban could not have been a more gungy Marine. He not only prided himself on his blade but also constantly strived to maintain the sharpest edge in all the Corps. Being half American Indian and Hispanic, knives were simply a way of life for Esteban, but none so much as his beloved K-Bar. During down time, which there is more than an abundance of in the hurry-up-and-wait environment of the Marine Corps, he'd pull his trusted blade from his non-regulation sheath depicting his culture and heritage and begin polishing it. Before long, a competition arose, and with it a fair share of ridicule from accidental slicing of flesh.

Days earlier, a young officer attempting to cut communication wire gashed into his own head as the fine-tuned blade bounced back at him while he looked closely at his target. Now, there are only a few things that bring happiness to grunts, and at the top is either seeing or hearing about how a young officer did something stupid, so this one certainly fit the bill. Of course, no one enjoyed embellishing the story more than Esteban. Yet, karma has a way of finding its own revenge.

Only hours after retelling the story during a chow break in a manner that had nearly every "Jar-rine" within earshot rolling on the floor, Esteban and his fellow knife-sharpening aficionados sat on the corner of their bunks, grinding away on their K-Bars. It was the infantryman's version of the "knitting circle," so to speak, while they waited for their next set of orders. After nearly a half-hour of sharpening, accompanied by the typical demonstrated machismo of slicing hairs from one's arm, the sergeant walked into the room and asked a simple question that would change the course of the day's events and get the lieutenant, who had recently gashed his head, off of the (ridicule) hook.

"So Esteban, you think your blade is a sharp as LT's?" The sergeant asked ("LT" being an accepted euphemism among experienced grunts to describe young lieutenants still finding their way in the military world).

"You mean this knife!" Esteban said in a loud, arrogant voice that echoed throughout the barracks as it captured everyone's attention.

What Esteban didn't know, at least not within the first few seconds, was that his enthusiastic burst of energy actually raised the blade from his thigh to his face with enough energy and momentum to allow the tip of the blade to nip into his nostril and cheek. Being the polished blade in the Corps, it easily and painlessly entered the skin, slicing deeply into the vascularity of his face.

Within seconds, blood started gushing from the wound, and Esteban experienced the metallic taste of blood pouring into this mouth.

"Holy shit!" a Marine belted out as he watched the free flow of blood start to pour like a faucet on high.

For a few seconds, some stood in amazement of how much blood can come from a small wound. Some watched with intrigue, but most just laughed. Before Esteban could get up and move to the head to wash his face and examine the wound, a big heavy hand slapped his forehead and forced him flat on the bunk. It was important the Marines immediately perform the first aid they'd been taught in infantry training school. A.B.C.'s, right? Meaning, address the patient's Airway, then Breathing, then Circulation. Well, maybe not. Although "Airway" is extremely important, hence being at the beginning of the acronym, it does not always need to be addressed or be addressed first. Esteban was already talking, or, in this case, cursing and screaming as if some alien had just landed on his face and caused all of this as to opposed to his pride in wanting to show off his sharp knife. Case in point is if the person is talking they've got a "patent airway" that is open and working fine. Of course, there is always the possibility that you may need to address it later.

While the guys thought they were following proper procedure by positioning Esteban flat on his back, they had actually made a grave mistake.

By keeping him in this position, they allowed the blood to flow from Esteban's nose and face into his mouth and throat, causing an obstruction and creating a problem that didn't previously exist. Man, despite all our stupidity, has evolved, and when placed in a survival situation, a human will automatically revert to primal instinct. As they held him down, Esteban fought to sit up in order to keep his airway open and give himself full vision of his surroundings. His condition was rapidly worsening as blood was now pouring into his mouth and eye sockets and soaking his hair. This relatively small wound was looking more like a life-threatening hemorrhage.

To make matters worse, as Esteban lay coughing up blood, even more hands began reaching in to place direct pressure over the wound. Usually, this is a good thing, but, when too much pressure is exerted and/or it obstructs an individual's airway, it can quickly compound a problem. Esteban began writhing around like a tightly wound rubber band that had just been released. A few of the Marines ripped open their battlefield medical kits and covered his face with bulk dressing so he looked like a mummy. Others pulled the blanket he was lying on from the rack to formulate a field-expedient stretcher.

By the time Esteban made it to treatment center, it appeared as if a chupacabra had attacked his face, and the rest of the Marines were forming hunting party to track it down and eat it. Marines can be enthusiastic at times. But, thankfully, cooler heads prevailed. Upon Esteban's arrival, the Hospital Corpsman or HM sat him up, unwrapped his face, and washed off the blood, debris, and other contamination that now had been introduced into the wound. They stuff-packed some gauze and maintained sufficient direct pressure over the wound in order to stop the bleeding. Fortunately, he was able to be back with the others to receive his share of ridicule by dinnertime.

Okay, so what went wrong? First off, don't be stupid, and treat anything that can hurt you with respect. Second, remove or mitigate the threat, which, in this case, was the K-Bar. Since no further injuries were incurred, I'd like to think someone picked it up and sheathed the culprit. If there is an auto accident, turn off the engine, and for an electrical incident, unplug the device. The bottom line is that you have to assess the situation and not simply react because it may be the last action you ever take. Third, A.B.C.'s works great for 99 percent of what you'll see, but if you're in a remote region with incredibly long transport time, you need to stop any major bleeding first. In special operations, we use MARCH as our casualty assessment, meaning stop Massive hemorrhage, and then address Airway, Respiration, Circulation, and Hypothermia. What good is having air flow if there's no blood to transport it to vital organs? However, in any other situation, take your own pulse first. Remain calm and stick to the A.B.C.'s. There are all sorts of medical kits available, and we've given you one here that will help any handyman to hunter, but it all comes down to the basics.

Assess the situation, get help, and remove any threats from doing more harm. Check for a patent airway, and if there's not one, make it by opening one for the patient. The "jaw thrust" is a must-know technique. This is done by placing your thumbs on the individual's cheeks and your fingertips behind their jaw. You apply pressure to push the jaw forward and open an airway. Look and feel for breathing. If they're not breathing or it is shallow or intermittent, it's not enough. Give rescue breathing because they will die without it. Stop the bleeding. This may require the use of a tourniquet, but most of the time, direct pressure, elevation, and pressure points can keep it under control until help arrives. Lastly, speak calmly and reassure the victim you are there for them. Just because they look unconscious doesn't mean they can't hear you. Human touch goes a long way and is something we all need to survive in life.

Emergency Situations

A lot of medicine, particularly emergency medicine, is not only about being equipped properly but also about being assertive. On a trip during my first deployment, I was the primary medic when we traveled to a country in South America. We were split up into groups of four staying in condominiums throughout the town. Even though I was the new guy, I insisted on bringing my medical gear home every night on the twenty-five-minute drive with traffic back from the military base where we were working. Since I had to pack all my gear—my trauma bag, a spine board, and O2—this made me the last guy to get in the truck every day. Because of this, I received plenty of crap from the other guys. SEALs don't like waiting on anyone, especially a new guy.

Then one night at about two in the morning, I heard a huge crash outside our condominium. I looked out into the street and saw there had been a terrible accident. A drunk cab driver had been driving too fast and slid sideways into a cement telephone pole. The car was ripped in half, and there were bodies spewed over the street.

The first thing Mark explained earlier in emergency situations is to make sure that you don't become part of the emergency situation, meaning you must make sure it is safe for you to proceed. As I made my way closer to the injured people in the street, I looked around to make sure there weren't any more drunk cab drivers racing around. Fortunately, there were not. The next thing you need to do in any type of stressful situation, particularly one that's going to call for emergency medical treatment, is to check your own pulse. I know Mark mentioned this also, but I can't stress it enough. This is to make sure you're not freaking out because, if that is the case, you're not going to be any help. Oddly enough, I was born without the "freak-out-when-things-are-going-bad" gene. I freak out plenty when things are really not that bad.

I quickly ran back up into my condo, grabbed my medical gear *that everyone was constantly bitching about*, and woke up my Teammates. Together, we went back downstairs in the street and started treating the injured people and stabilizing them. There were a total of four patients and they were pretty badly hurt—open compound fractures of the femur, spinal injuries, and head wounds. Although it was a very graphic sight, I was trained and equipped for the situation. I realized some of the people might die if they didn't get more definitive treatment, so we got our vehicles together, secured them in the back, and drove them back to the Naval base that we were working out of.

When we arrived at the base, I was assertive and made the guard recall the medical staff because I knew it was the right thing to do. In the end, they came in and really saved the day.

I think that was the second Navy Achievement Medal I received, and I was proud about that one.

The important thing to remember is that there are some basic steps to take every time there is an emergency, medical or not. Make sure you're going to be okay, and make sure your surroundings are safe, meaning you're not going to get hit by a bus, electrocuted, or—in combat—shot. If you are in combat and a guy gets shot, there is a reason he got hit at that specific location, so it is important to approach with caution when you attempt to render aid. The situation may even call for you to maybe throw a couple smoke grenades. In a civilian context, if a bear attacked a person you might want to look and listen for the animal before you run over to help, preferably with a large gun. If you are in a remote area, look for massive hemorrhage, and then check the airway, check the breathing, and do regular circulation, meaning stop all "little" bleeding, then immobilize the fractures.

I guarantee that the one time you need medical supplies and don't have them, you will remember it as a negative incident for the rest of your life. Do yourself a favor and keep important supplies on hand. Don't be that guy.

Based on the most common injuries and sports related injuries in the US, here is a list of items that would be good for a medical kit for three different uses.

General Medical Kit (listed below)
Sportsman/Hunter's Kit
Soccer Mom/Family Kit

Quantity/Item

1 Compression Bandage
1 Compressed Gauze (Wrap)
1 Elastic Wrap (ACE) Velcro Close
1 Cravat Bandage
4 Large Band-Aids, Knuckle
4 Band-Aids, Standard
1 Exam Gloves
1 CPR Face Shield
1 Mini-Trauma Shears/Scissors
1 Betadine Swab
1 Medic Reinforcement Tape
2 Large Safety Pins
1 Antibiotic Ointment
1 Pain Reliever (Acetaminophen/Tylenol pkg)
1 Anti-inflammatory (Ibuprofen/Motrin pkg)
1 12"x12" Zip Closure Bag (Ice)
1 Heat Retention Space Blanket

These kits can be found at: www.battlereadymedic.com

CHAPTER VII

In And Around The House

You often hear people say owning a home is an essential part of the American Dream, and I also believe this to be partially true. Knowing that you're putting your feet down on *your* earth is something that is difficult to describe, but being an American is not defined by material objects; it is an idea. However, having a home and land makes you feel like you have something tangible to pass on to your children, that there is evidence of your existence. As with all things that are worth having, owning a home is a big responsibility. Even if you are independently wealthy, keeping your home and land requires your time.

Home Repair

While fixing your home can sometimes be fun and rewarding, it can also be endlessly frustrating—sort of like an afternoon trip to the DMV in California. Let's first talk about plumbing and electricity because they tend to present the biggest problems. Here is my advice when it comes to these areas: Hire a professional. You will ask: "Why spend the extra money to have a qualified individual come to your home?" The simple answer is: The odds are you don't know what you are doing. You may think you do, but *you do not*. Sure, you may have watched half a dozen how-to videos on YouTube, but these only take you so far.

Despite your best intentions, you may very well end up lighting yourself on fire, or burning down your house, flooding it, or electrocuting yourself.

Back in 2005, we were in a residential neighborhood in Baghdad when some local genius attempted to tap into the grid to get free power for his house. This is not unusual there or in other countries. If you have ever visited Tijuana, Mexico, you will see evidence of the same urban ingenuity. It's really is not that difficult to do because you basically run cables from the power lines or junction box to the line running to your home. In Mexico, they prefer to use bent forks to hook over the lines. It's not rocket surgery. So, this joker went to the junction box right across the street from the house we were responsible for and tried to tap into it with some type of electrical conductive object. To be honest, I don't know what he was trying to use. And the thing is, no one will ever know because he stuck whatever was in his hand into the junction box and got zapped with about a gazillion volts and amps. It ended up being the last mistake he would make on this planet because he essentially disintegrated in a *boom* and a flash of light. All we found were burnt pieces of clothing and some scorched Iraqi dinars, which is the national currency.

There is a reason these guys and gals go through years of school and apprenticeship to become certified in their trade. Let the professionals do what they do best.

However, once you have called the pro, watch them closely. Get right over their shoulder as they work and ask plenty of questions. You're paying them for their expertise, so why not educate yourself along the way. I recently learned the hard way that I would have been better off consulting a professional when I un-winterized my farm in northern Wisconsin. As the farm is nearly in Canada, if you are going to leave a property like this vacant for any time in the colder months, it is necessary either to keep the house heated while you are gone or "winterize" it. This means draining all of the water out of everything in the house in order to prevent the plumbing from freezing and bursting. This means *everything*, the toilet bowls, water lines, and the water heater. To finish the job, you have to hook an air compressor to blow that last bits of air out of the system.

When we went to reoccupy the farm, I reversed the process of winterizing, but did not realize that the water heater had to be completely full *before* you powered it up again. Several hours and $300 later, we had hot water again. The bottom line from electricity and plumbing: It is worth getting to know solid professionals in both of these fields in your local area. Learn from them, and then go forth and do great things.

Barbecuing and Grilling

My mother-in-law has always said that the best cooks are men. I don't really track that stuff, but, traditionally speaking, in America, guys really didn't "cook,"

But grilling and barbecuing are another story.

This is the most ancient method of cooking known to man. Fire + Meat = Great. Fire + Meat + Beer + Friendship = Awesome. When we talk about fire and meat, some people don't realize there is a difference between barbecuing and grilling: Barbecuing is the slower of the two and involves the meat not coming into direct contact with the flame, while grilling relies on direct heat to cook your food much more quickly.

The man I have chosen to tell you about barbecuing is Kelly Mulligan. When Kelly was eighteen or so, and I was about ten, he lived with my brother, mother, and me, in our basement. We lived in a small, rural southern Wisconsin town, named Hartland. This was during the 1970s, and Kelly was a good-looking guy with naturally curly hair that looked like a permanent who regularly played Billy Squier and REO Speedwagon down in his basement pad, which was pretty sweet. When I was growing up, Kelly was all that was man. When he used to get gussied up to go out and meet his friends, I would watch him in awe. When he put his cologne on, he would rub it onto his hands, pat it onto his face, and then take a little dab and put it right over his belly button, laugh, and say, "One for the ladies."

It took me about fifteen years to figure out what Kelly was talking about, and when I did, it only made me think he was that much cooler. He turned out to be one of the most squared-away human beings that have ever lived. He eventually found his "lady" in, Nida, his wife, and it turns out he is the best barbecuer I've ever met.

Grilling

By Kelly Mulligan

Kellymulliganinsurance.com

Owner Kelly Mulligan Insurance

Grilling is a useful craft that all men should learn. My first exposure to grilling was when I was a young boy. My dad had a fixed-post (stationary) natural gas grill. One of my favorite foods my dad grilled was hamburgers with BBQ sauce. Wow—how things have changed since those days!

My first grill, as an adult, was a Sears Kenmore™ gas grill. It was not anything fancy, and flare-ups occurred easily. Before too long, the food had an unintended extra crunch. As I learned how to grill, my family endured many over-cooked meals.

My grilling skills have improved greatly since the days of the Sears Kenmore, and I have experimented with many types of grills over the years. I moved from the Sears gas grill, to a Weber™ Kettle grill, to a Weber gas grill, then back to the Weber Kettle grill. Currently, I have two gas grills: one Weber Kettle, and, my favorite, the Big Green Egg™. The Big Green Egg is undeniably the best and most versatile grill I have ever used. It is a ceramic grill that is somewhat egg-shaped, hence the name. This grill works great for basic grilling such as burgers, steaks, and brats. The versatility of it also makes it a favorite for more advanced foods such as pork, beef brisket, pizzas, bread, and dessert. My favorite food to grill on the Big Green Egg is slow-cooked baby back ribs.

One unique feature of the Big Green Egg is its fuel source—lump charcoal, which is a carbonized hardwood. Adding different woods provides additional flavor to the food being grilled. I keep a supply of hickory, apple, mesquite, pimento, and guava woods on hand for a variety of flavor options.

Another feature of the Big Green Egg is its ability to hold a steady temperature from 200 degrees to 650 degrees, which enables cooking a variety of foods.

Grilling gives men the opportunity to bond. Recently, I was riding my bike through a city park, and I noticed a group of people at the pavilion. All ages and genders were part of this group of people. However, one thing stood out as I rode by: Six men were standing around the park grill. I'm not sure how a grill creates such an attraction to men. Maybe it's the smell of burning wood. Maybe it's the chance to have a few beers and share a few laughs with the guys. For any men who have never grilled before, I would encourage you to give it a try. Sure, you might ruin a few meals along the way, but you will have fun in the process.

Quick Tips:

1. A good insta-read meat thermometer is worth its weight in gold. Get one and use it.
2. Keep your grill at a cooler temperature rather than a hotter one. It is easier to increase the heat when cooking than decrease.
3. Be sure to make slight adjustments on the dampeners—no radical changes.
4. Season your meats with dry spices instead of liquid marinades.
5. Spend more money for higher-quality cuts of meat.
6. Make sure you cook to the right temperature. Temperatures for veal, beef, lamb steaks and roasts:

Rare	Soft with a red center	125–130 °F
Medium rare	A warm red center	130–140 °F
Medium	Firm with a pink center	140–150 °F
Medium well	A small amount of pink in the center	150–155 °F
Well done	Firm throughout	160 °F+

Then, take your meat off of the grill and let it sit for ten minutes before serving.

SEALs and BBQs

Stay with me here; this really does pertain to a BBQ.

If SEALs are ever in a fight with somebody and they grab our rifle, we're just going to give it to them. Now, granted, it's got a sling, so they're not going to run away with it, but as soon as someone puts their hands on your rifle in an attempt to take it, they are now considered "armed," and you can kill them. So, while they are focusing on it, you reach down, grab your pistol, and shoot them.

I can only imagine what is going through the mind of a guy that has worked himself up enough to grab a SEAL's rifle. Maybe he puts on a cool uniform or maybe he doesn't. Maybe he decides to dress like a civilian in an attempt to gain an advantage. Then he thinks to himself, "Hey, I'm going to get in a fight with those SEALs," and finally gets close enough to one of them where he actually grabs a hold of a rifle. He is probably thrilled...for a moment. Until he tries to actually pull the gun away, and the next thing he knows his brain is on the wall behind him. I think that would be rather disappointing.

Something very similar to a scenario like this happened in Iraq when some SEALs raided a house. During the process, a very large man bum-rushed one of the guys, knocked him on his back, and was trying to pull his rifle away from him as they were on the kitchen floor. When you are in the middle of an assault such as this, you're on your own if the other guys were busy. In this case, they were. When the SEAL got knocked onto his back, he slid underneath a sink from the momentum. This isn't like a typical sink you would picture in your mind; it was more in the style of an old-time washroom sink where there are two legs and then a basin above. The SEAL found himself underneath the sink with the two legs under his armpits, preventing him from being able to climb out *or* reach his pistol.

As he was trying to fight the Iraqi guy and get out from underneath the sink, his hands moved around and eventually found a little metal hibachi grill. Without access to his rifle or his pistol, he grabbed the metal hibachi and smashed the guy on the head with it. This knocked the guy off of him, and he was able to slide out from under the sink and wrap the guy up.

This is, bar none, the coolest barbecuing story I have ever heard.

Butchering a Chicken

I think it's safe to say that a lot of guys really have no idea how to butcher a chicken any longer. And why would they? Today, you can go to almost any grocery store and purchase a butchered chicken. You can buy a whole "fryer," which are typically about five pounds or larger and is the complete bird with the skin intact, but it's been gutted and no longer has a head or feet. More likely than not some of the internal organs—the heart, gizzard, neck, and liver—will be inside the cavity of the bird in a small bag.

So why should you be able to butcher a chicken when you can simply buy one?

One, you get to cut up the bird as you choose, and, two, practice. Butchering an uncooked chicken is just like carving a chicken to serve for dinner or a turkey for Thanksgiving.

If you're going to make fried chicken, you generally do not cook it whole unless you're deep frying it. As I really enjoy fried chicken, and I think you should be able to make fried chicken as a man, we will go through the steps. But, first, let me tell you how disappointing it can be when the bird is not prepared properly.

When I was in Vietnam doing the unclassified Joint Task Force—Full Accounting mission, we made our way back up to Hanoi after searching for an F-4 Phantom that had crashed in the jungle. On the way, we went to a restaurant where they had what appeared to be rotisserie chicken, which is, as most of you know, where they take the chicken, stick it on a metal rod, and spin it around really slowly to cook it. We had been out in the middle of nowhere eating chicken lips and snake assholes, so I was starving. Once I saw the chicken on the rotisserie, it was all I could think of eating.

When I pointed to the chicken, the woman working at the restaurant smiled back at me. Her teeth were black from chewing betel nut, a mildly narcotic stimulant, which is crushed and eaten with lye—yes, it's kind of weird. I can't say that it is at all appetizing to see someone with black teeth prepare my food, but I was hungry.

I looked on as the woman grabbed the chicken and set it on a cutting board in front of me. I couldn't wait to be served a delicious meal. But instead of pulling out a sharp, non-serrated carving knife, she held out a meat cleaver and quickly started bashing the chicken, shattering its bones, and turning everything into a bony chicken pulp. Needless to say, I was devastated...but still incredibly hungry. It still tasted like chicken, but it had lost its appeal. There is a world of difference when you butcher a chicken the correct way.

Occasionally, my family had our reunions down in Luverne, Minnesota, the little farming community in the southwest part of the state. During these get-togethers, we had to feed about three thousand people. Fortunately, a few of my uncles still lived there and had farms, where they raised chickens and other animals.

During one trip, my cousin Patrick and I went over to my Uncle Gene's place with the instructions that we were going to slaughter and clean some chickens. After some thought, Patrick and I came up with our grand plan of how to do this. We got a tree stump, drove two nails into the top of it about an inch and a half apart, and left them about two inches sticking up to make a little trap. Our plan was to grab the chickens, stick their heads in between these two nails, stretch their necks out, cut their heads off, and then throw them behind us. This is how the execution would take place.

It all hinged on us first catching the chickens—and they are *fast*. Anyone who has seen the movie *Rocky* knows this. The best way we found was to get a coat hanger, untwist it so it becomes one long piece of wire, put a bend at the end of it, and then run behind the chicken and swing it under its legs. Don't do it hard, you're not trying to torture the bird, but you whip the wire and pull it toward you. The bend or slight hook that you've made will wind up catching on the chicken's foot and allow you to pull it toward you and grab it with your hand.

Patrick and I were doing our best to reach our goal of thirty chickens, but the process was taking a long time. Eventually, our Grandma Esther Mulligan, a tough farm lady, came out of the house to check on us.

"What in the heck are you doing?" She asked.

"Killing these chickens, Grandma," I told her.

"So, what's taking so long?"

When Patrick and I showed her the method we'd been using, Grandma just stared at us for a minute then sprang into action.

In one smooth movement, she grabbed the coat hanger, whipped it under a chicken, pulled the chicken up, grabbed it, put her hand on the chicken's head, wrung its neck, and then pulled a knife out of somewhere and cut that chicken's head off. This entire maneuver took about three seconds. Grandma could put any gang member to shame and was essentially a farming ninja and a known serial killer of chickens. Patrick and I stood looking on with our mouths open and jaws on the ground, realizing for the hundredth time that we should never, ever screw with Grandma Mulligan.

However you choose to remove the chicken's head, it's a good idea to get it off because, otherwise, the rest of this will not go very well. Once its nervous system has settled down—they will flop around vigorously for a bit—take it by the feet, dip it into boiling water, and then start pulling the feathers off. There's no real fun way to do this. Commercial machines look similar to a washing machine, but they have black rubber fingers on the inside of the drum. Once you put a chicken in there, it rapidly spins around and knocks the feathers off. It's remarkable, but if you don't have one of those, you're just going to have to do it the old-fashioned way.

Once you have removed the feathers, it is best to have a cutting board and a fairly sharp knife. You can also have what are known as poultry scissors to assist in butchering the chicken. The first thing you want to do is set the chicken on its back so you can look at it and get a grasp of the anatomy of the bird. There should be two wings, two legs, a breast, thighs connected to the legs, and a back. There's also something called the "Pope's nose," which is actually the tail of the bird. I'm not sure which Pope had a nose that looked like a chicken ass, but I'm pretty sure he wasn't happy about this nickname. Anyway, it stuck.

When the chicken is on its back, you'll notice that the area underneath the breastbone sags down a little bit—this is where the guts are. Take your sharp knife, tent the skin up with your fingers, and make an incision in the abdomen. Once you have done this, open it up, reach in, and pull those guts out. Once you get the majority of the guts out, it is good to run it under cold water and then scrape your thumbnail along the back side of the spine and the ribs to get out any coagulated blood or other bits that may be stuck in there. When all this is done, go ahead and pat the chicken dry with some paper towels, or dish towels if you're environmentally conscious. You'll just have to wash them later.

Once the chicken's dry, pick it up by what remains of the neck. If you move it around a little bit, you'll see exactly where you need to cut to remove it. The process of butchering this chicken is, in a medical term, called "dis-articulation." What we're going to do is focus on where the things are connected. Like I said, we're going to start with the neck, so look and see where the neck is actually connected to the body. This is where you're going to cut the neck, right on the top of the chicken. Be careful not to stab yourself.

The next thing you can do to make this bird look a little bit more like one you buy in the grocery store is to remove the feet. You'll notice that the skin on the chicken foot is yellow and sort of scaly right up to what would be an ankle joint. Feel this with your fingers, take you knife and poke it in between the two sides of the joint, and then slowly make a circumferential cut around the joint. You will find there will be a couple tendons, but cut those too, and remove the feet completely. If you've ever been to Chinatown in San Francisco, or really any Chinatown in any large city, or I would assume a town in China itself—although I've never been to China—you may want to save the feet to cook. I have never eaten a chicken foot, so I'm not sure how they would be, but making that choice is up to you. Now, if you set your bird down, it really looks like a typical whole fryer that you would find in the grocery store.

With the chicken still positioned flat on its back, you'll notice where the leg is hinged when you reach down and flip it outward. If this were a person it would essentially be the hip joint. Run your fingers along the back side of the leg until you feel a groove where the leg is actually attached to the body itself.

Once again, tent the skin along that line and make a little incision so you can stick your finger inside. That's the separation of what would be the thigh to the torso. Take your knife and cut all the way around, roughly following that line. You'll eventually get down to the hip joint itself, and, after you do, grab the leg by the thigh and push it up and out. It should make a little cracking noise and start to separate. At that point, take your knife, and, like you did to remove the foot, cut in between the joint. It should come off cleanly.

You now have the leg and the thigh removed from the bird. Do the same thing on the opposite side.

Now go up to the wings. You'll notice that what would be the shoulder is similar to what we just did with the hip of the bird. Rock it back and forth so you're identifying exactly where that joint is, and then make a small incision after you tent the skin. After you perform a circumferential cut around there, you should be able to pop the joint by going up and outwards. As you did with the leg, make the final cut with your knife to separate the wing. Then, repeat this procedure on the other side.

Now, in front of you, you should have two wings by themselves, two legs and thighs connected, and the remainder of the upper and lower torso of the bird. Looking at the torso as it sits on the cutting board, you'll follow the angle of the breast, which goes back in a V towards what used to be the location of the head. You'll notice that there is some skin and very thin muscle keeping it connected to the back. Make an incision along that angle with your knife, making sure that you don't cut into the breastbone…or your finger. Once you get to the top of the bird, simply grab the breast that is almost completely severed and the back of the bird and pry it apart. You can bet there will be plenty of crackling noises and whatnot, but don't be afraid. The bird can't feel anything, so take your knife and complete the cut. This is a great place to use your poultry scissors. Save the back to boil for chicken stock.

At this point, you pretty much have the bird divided up. If you feel along the top of the breast, there will be a little ridge that's running along the mid line. That's called the "sternum." Pick a side and run your knife right next to the sternum, all the way down to the breastbone, and give it one final chop. You can also use a meat cleaver for this, but I'm willing to bet that your meat cleaver skills aren't that great. Instead, this is also where you can use your poultry shears, so cut the flesh down to the breastbone, and then simply snip the rest of the way.

Voila, you have two chicken breasts.

Getting back to the legs: Pick one up, and rock it back and forth holding the thigh in one hand and the leg in the other hand. That'll clearly identify where the knee joint is. Put your finger on it and feel the gap between the bones. This is where you run your knife circumferentially around it, then take the two and pop them apart. Again, you'll have a little bit of flesh left and some tendons to cut, but that is all.

Once you're proficient in this, it should take about five minutes—in addition to the time it takes to kill, pluck, and clean—to have this bird completely done. That's it. Ready to be fried.

Carving a Bird

Thanksgiving is one of my favorite times of year and also, oddly enough, only an American holiday. I say "oddly" because, until you travel outside of the country during Thanksgiving, you probably never realized this. When my entire family lived in Germany, we had some friends that were local Germans; their last name is Wolf, pronounced "Volf"… Martin, Doris, Alex, and Katarina. My wife, Sara, became friends with Doris through the Black Forest Quilters' Guild, and the Wolfs were what would be known as a typical German family. Actually, they would be known as "very typical Schwäbian" as they are from Baden-Württemberg, Germany. Martin was a civil servant, and Doris was an office worker. The kids went to school. They were an incredibly nice family.

It was so fantastic to have the Wolfs over to our small, four-bedroom apartment for an American Thanksgiving. Thanksgiving symbolizes abundance. However, if you look at the average American and the average German, you'll see that the Americans are quite a bit heavier than the Germans, so it could easily also symbolize gluttony. Quite frankly, I don't care because I love Thanksgiving. It is the best, and I believe that it is now the Wolfs' favorite American holiday also.

Eating turkey appears to be culturally associated with America. The Wolfs had never had a roasted turkey before, and, when you pull that bird out, it looks amazing if you have never seen a turkey cooked that way because you are just expecting a chicken. As you know, aside from the larger size, a turkey looks similar to a chicken when they don't have any feathers. What do you do once this beautiful turkey is cooked?

Carve it up.

I have never seen, ever, in any of my forty-five Thanksgivings—of which I could probably remember, I don't know, twenty of them—anyone hand a woman a carving knife and fork. It only seems that a guy gets handed the knife in order to carve the bird.

And if you happen to be that guy, and you have never done this before, it could be very intimidating. It is Thanksgiving, and there is a crowd of family and friends awaiting the juicy main dish of the meal. From the moment you are handed the carving knife, you are under the gun. Thankfully, you have read the previous section in this chapter and know how to dis-articulate a chicken. Carving a turkey is nearly identical, but we are going to start in a different order.

First, look at the top of the bird and identify the sternum, the point right in the middle of the breast. Take your very sharp, non-serrated knife, and—directly to the left and to the right of the sternum—run it straight down until it hits the rib cage. Then, take the knife and turn it parallel to the table, about a quarter of an inch below the top of the breast, on either the left or the right side; take your pick. Now, slowly cut into it until the knife reaches the sternum. Repeat this process, moving downward, slicing the breast to your desired thickness. Do this until you reach the rib cage and, at that point, the only thing you'll have to do is slightly angle the knife up to get the rest of the meat. Other than that, removing the legs, separating the leg from the thigh, and removing the wings is exactly the same as when butchering a chicken.

I would encourage you to practice your carving skills prior to Thanksgiving, several times if possible.

Cooking Eggs

Eggs are not only fantastic but also can be any single man's best friend. People mostly choose to eat chicken eggs, but there are also other kinds such as duck, ostrich, and quail, which are quite delicious. In Asia, I used to hang out with the locals and occasionally drink rice whiskey and eat hardboiled quail eggs, which are about the size of your thumbnail. It's a nice way to pass the time. Granted, the rice whiskey's absolutely horrible, but it's pretty hard to explain that to somebody about their national drink because they tend to get a little testy.

Eggs are different grades and sizes. The more A's there are, the higher the quality. For instance, a grade triple A is better than a grade A. Let me tell you one thing, though, when you're picking out your eggs: Don't forget to open up the carton. You don't have to pull out each egg and inspect the bottom, but if you lightly flick it with your finger, you will be able to tell if the shell has cracked because it will stick in place. The egg white leaks out and glues the shell to the inside of the carton. Make sure you check your eggs because, otherwise, you're going to be unhappy when you return home from the store to find you wound up paying for twelve eggs and can only use ten.

As a rule of thumb, if the egg is refrigerated when you buy it, you should refrigerate it afterward as well. If it's not refrigerated when you buy it, you should not have to refrigerate it. Now, granted, these eggs are not fertilized. If an egg is fertilized, it'll start to grow the embryo inside of it. Again, in Asia, duck and chicken eggs that are fertilized and have partially developed embryos are considered a delicacy. In the Philippines, it's called balut, and it is not all that bad if you can get past the crunchy part of their beaks and little feet. I bet by now you have guessed that they actually taste like chicken or duck. They do smell a bit, though; however, I encourage you to give it a try if you ever travel to these countries and have an opportunity to sit down and eat with these folks. If you vomit, then you vomit, but it is a great way to learn and experience the local culture.

Back in America, there are a few different ways that you will most likely prepare eggs. They can be divided into preparation methods that use water and those that do not use water. You will boil them or fry them in the morning for breakfast. Do not microwave an egg unless you are into cleaning the inside of microwaves. It will not blow up and destroy your kitchen, but it will pop and spatter egg everywhere inside it. Boiling eggs at specific temperatures for certain amounts of time leads to a distinct result. If you like an egg runny, it's called soft-boiled, and this usually takes two minutes in boiling water. You start the time when you add the eggs into boiling water. The result is the yolk is still runny, but the white is solid. Use the side of a small spoon to crack and remove the pointed end of the egg, making a hole in the shell large enough to fit the spoon. If you don't like the egg runny, you can go with a medium-boiled egg, which will take approximately four and a half minutes, and the yolk will be dense in the middle but still dark orange-yellow in color and moist. You can also choose to cook the egg for about eight minutes until it is hard-boiled, which leaves the yolk light yellow, completely solid, and crumbly. If you make the mistake of leaving it in the boiling water for too long, you will notice a green or gray ring around the yolk, so be sure to set a timer and keep an eye on the stove.

The other type of preparation of eggs with water is called "poaching." You do this by using something that looks like a muffin tin for making muffins, but it's much shallower and rounded on the bottom. What you do is set this in a pan full of water, crack the eggs open, place them inside, and let them cook.

A fried egg is just that—an egg that is fried. When I lived in Africa—I think you know what's coming next—it's hot. I was at my house one day when the temperature was somewhere around 125 degrees outside. I took a piece of aluminum sheeting, like the kind of stuff you find in an air duct, and set it down outside on the ground. I took an egg, cracked it, and opened it up over the top of this piece of aluminum sheeting. No kidding, it fried. Then I stopped for a minute to think of how stupid that was to waste an egg. But I had to do it. I guarantee you, if you ever visit Africa, and you have the chance, you will fry an egg just like that.

There are three basic ways to do this in your kitchen at home. With all of them, you're going to start with the pan at a medium-high to high temperature and covered with some type of lubrication. I prefer vegetable oil. There are so many different types of oil, the only one you *cannot* use is labeled "motor oil." If you want to have the most available yolk for dipping your toast, for instance, which is a Midwestern farm thing, you would most likely choose to cook your egg sunny side up. This is where you crack the egg, open it up, and let it fall into the pan. The yolk looks like a sun, and it's facing up, hence the name. Once the egg hits the pan, it will immediately start to fry, so be careful because the oil may spatter. Take your spatula, and gently slide it underneath the egg to make sure it doesn't stick to the pan. Once it's cooked as much as you would like, you can remove it. You can also take a spoon, or your spatula, and splash a little of the hot oil on top of the egg itself, to help cook the membrane. You'll know it's cooking when it starts to turn white.

Another style is called "over easy," which gives you a little less uncooked yolk volume, but also takes care of that pesky-looking, slimy mucus membrane that's on top of the sunny side up egg. Follow the same procedures: hot pan, oil, crack the egg, and let it fry for a bit. As soon as it becomes stiff enough for you to get the spatula underneath without ripping it, quickly flip it over. Let it cook for about twenty to thirty seconds, just enough to get that membrane done, then remove it and eat. A third type is called "over medium." It's exactly the same thing as over easy, only you let it cook a little longer. I'm sorry; there is a fourth way. It is called "cooking the crap out of the egg." This is generally used for fried egg sandwiches. Put the egg in the pan, pop the yoke, and cook the crap out of it. Done.

The final way to prepare eggs with a pan and without water is scrambling. In order to do this, take your eggs, find a bowl, and crack them open. Put them in the bowl, get a fork, and whip them up. That's it, man. No kidding.

Here is an actual useful note from the lawyer: "As an aside, there is a lot more to making good scrambled eggs. These instructions are completely inadequate." I had no idea this dude was a scrambled egg aficionado. He took the time on the phone to describe, from memory, the proper techniques and temperature for cooking the perfect scrambled eggs. I think the only thing that could make him more upset than me not listing these details would be missing an ambulance to chase.

The real reason I did not get into the scrambled egg thing too deeply is that I still have problems eating them since Navy boot camp. I may need therapy now just thinking about this. It just occurred to me that I should sue my lawyer for pain and suffering.

Bread

Mike and Lorrie Roeder have been friends of mine since I've known my wife, and they have been family friends with the Whitelocks, my wife's family, since she was a young girl. The Roeders are an incredibly interesting and fun couple, and I am telling you right now if you ever get an invitation to their house for dinner, stop whatever you are planning on doing, and take them up on it. Lorrie is a fantastic hostess, and Mike is one heck of a good cook.

If you didn't know Mike and met him for the first time, you might say he is a bit of an odd bird. This is why: He is one of those guys that, whatever he decides to do, he does it to an incredibly high standard. I'll give you an example. Mike had a buddy that used to fix his watches, and when he decided to retire from his work, Mike said, "Hey, I wouldn't mind doing that." So he acquired the guy's entire set of tools and spare parts and set up a watch repair shop in his basement. Because he is so fantastically good at whatever he decides to do, people from around the world ship him their watches to fix.

Here is another example. For quite a few years, Mike has been collecting beautiful religious Orthodox Christian icons. Again, with anything Mike does, he decides to go completely overboard with it, starts getting these fantastic icons from around the world, and then he builds a display case…well, "case" is not the right word; it is just a beautiful display inside of his living room. Mike thought of this ingenious thing where he took copper piping, cut little windows out that faced the icons, and then put lighting inside so you could alter their appearance. When you go into Mike's living room, it is like walking into a museum.

I asked Mike to be in this book for a couple of reasons. One, the bread that he is about to explain how to make is absolutely delicious. But two, Mike symbolizes something to me which is very important about being a man, and that is anything worth doing is worth *over-doing*. Men should not be just experts. Men should be experts in becoming experts and that, to me, summarizes Mike perfectly.

Baking Bread

By Mike Roeder

When Mike is not baking, he is fixing cars, repairing watches, collecting Russian icons, or watching whales off the coast of California. It's an eccentric retirement, contrasting web surfing with ocean exploring, fine motor skills with sun exposure, but it suits him. If you want to know more, read his recent book called *One Thousand Whales in One Year* which you can easily find at 1kin1yr.com or the iBook store.

I started baking about fifteen years ago when I decided I needed to contribute more to the world other than a collection of scruffy cars, *and* I needed to improve my diet. Bread is an ancient, manly creation based on simple ingredients combined with a dose of smarts and hard work. It involves measuring, calculating, making a bit of a mess, precision equipment, and fire. Eventually, it gets combined with meat, cheese, wine, butter, and sharp knives. What's not to like?

Bread is both simple and complex. My recipe is easy enough for anyone to grasp. The only thing that surprises folks is the time involved. Why so much time? Because we are coaxing millions of tiny yeast creatures to do all of the hard work for us.

Here's the recipe I've refined, on a sheet of paper stuck to my refrigerator door:

Water (16 oz., 1 lb., or 450 grams)
Flour (20 oz., 1.25 lb., or 570 grams)
Yeast (1/2 teaspoon)
Salt (1 tablespoon)

Here's the process: (Don't change it!)

7. Pour lukewarm water in
    a big plastic tub.

8. Sprinkle in the yeast and
    wait a minute.

9. Dump in good white bread flour.

10. Sprinkle the salt on top.

11. Mix with a big spoon
    for 25 strokes.

12. Cover the tub with a clean
    damp towel.

13. Put in a warm place and wait
    8-12 hours.

14. Sprinkle a bit of flour
    on a counter.

15. Coax the dough out with
    the big spoon.

16. Gently shape the dough
    into a ball.

17. Oil the inside of a glass
    or metal bowl.

18. Set dough inside and
    cover with towel.

19. Wait 90-120 min while
    it rises again.

20. Heat oven to 450° F (230° C).

21. Put your bowl in the oven.

22. Bake for 10-15 minutes.

23. Turn down heat to
    400° F (200° C).

24. Bake 35-45 minutes.

25. Remove from bowl, set on
    rack in oven.

26. Cool 1 hour, cut, and eat.

Like most things in life, you can complicate bread making. Add ingredients like sugar, oil, milk, and seeds. Demand that I take out the salt. Insist we must all be gluten-free. Well, I'm sorry for your medical conditions, but many centuries of refinement have determined that BREAD is flour, water, yeast, and salt, plus time and heat. Not the chemical fabrication our stores insist is bread. Give up something else instead, but stick to reality in your basic foundations of living.

My Bread Experience

I'm sure you know by now that I like getting to understand cultures through food. In 2006, I was in Baghdad walking around the back of a house on our compound that was used by some of our coalition partners as both a bunk house and a cook house, when I noticed what looked like a washing machine hooked up to a tank of gas. Being the inquisitive type, I went up and grabbed the Iraqi who spoke no English and started pointing to this thing and asking him what it was. He walked me up to it, and I looked inside. It was empty, but the gas tank was connected to the side of it, and in the space of the walls, which were about three inches apart, there were vents for the gas to come in. When you lit the gas, it heated the tub uniformly around the circle.

I still wasn't grasping the purpose of this appliance, so the Iraqi took me inside the kitchen where his buddy had about thirty-five or forty little dough balls. Next to them was something that looked like a small pillow with a handle on the back of it. He then put a bunch of the dough balls on a board and walked outside with them and the pillow. I followed. After flattening out one of the dough balls, he stuck it on the pillow, and then grabbed it on the other side with the handle. In a quick movement, he put his hand inside the washing-machine-looking appliance, which was about seven thousand degrees by then, and thrust the pillow with the dough at the sidewall. Looking on as this all took place, I quickly realized this was the process with which they cooked their flat bread.

I tried this a couple of times and ended up burning myself and some bread, but after about twenty-five minutes, I learned how to cook it like an Iraqi.

There you have it. War may be hell, but at least you have bread.

Mustangs and Pizza

Todd Braden has been a friend of mine for a long time, since I moved to Oregon from the Midwest and started my freshman year of high school. During those days, I wore bandannas around my neck and essentially had a mullet haircut. The Pacific Northwest is remarkably different from the Midwest even though they are just one part of a word separated. Todd was one of the cool kids in town and had a Ford Mustang 5.0, which was a big deal back then. It was white with beige interior.

One night, we had been out doing whatever, hooting with the owls and drinking beer. Both of us were a little slippy, me more than him, and we smoked cigarettes.

Todd was driving me back to my house in his Mustang along this little, two-lane road in Lake Oswego, Oregon when we both decided we wanted a smoke. Unfortunately, we had locked the pack in the glove box for some reason. I'm sure they have changed this by now, but you used to be able to pull the key out of the Mustang's ignition as you were driving, and the car would continue to run.

"Todd, man, the glove box is locked," I told him. "Give me the keys."

Even though we were traveling along at around forty miles per hour, Todd popped the keys out of the ignition and handed them to me. I started to unlock the glove box but fumbled around a little bit as we approached a slight curve in the road. At this point, Todd turned the wheel to stay on the road, but there was a problem. You may or may not know this already, but I will pass on this knowledge anyway— if you turn the steering wheel of a car with no key in the ignition, one of the things manufacturers have done is install a locking mechanism. So, once Todd turned the wheel, it stayed locked in place.

"Give me the keys back," Todd said. "I need to unlock the wheel!"

As we were nearing the bend, I was still trying to unlock the glove box in order to get the cigarettes when we started to drift off of the road. And then I *dropped* the keys onto the floor.

Todd again tried to move the steering wheel, but it wasn't going anywhere, and we started peeling off the side of the road. The entire situation was like watching a train wreck in slow motion. As I was a future Navy SEAL, you could probably guess what happened next: I immediately identified the keys on the floor, picked them up, separated the right key, inserted it into the ignition, grabbed the steering wheel, and pulled us back on the road mere seconds before we ran into the ditch!

But if you guessed this, you are absolutely wrong.

I continued to mess around, trying to grab the keys on the floor, until I found myself looking up and becoming mesmerized by the white line on the side of the road. It started to move farther and farther towards the center of Todd's Mustang…and kept in that direction until we dropped off a ledge. Thankfully, it was only about a three-and-a-half-foot embankment, and, by this time, Todd had us almost completely stopped by applying the brakes. But we still drove his beautiful new Mustang 5.0 into a ditch.

Immediately upon hitting the side of the car into the trees, I picked up the keys, put them into the lock on the glove box, opened it, pulled out two cigarettes, and lit them.

Mission accomplished.

After we got the car out of the ditch, Todd went on to get married, have some kids, and open several pizza restaurants in the Portland, Oregon area. We are still friends to this day. And, in case you are wondering, Todd and I both quit smoking years ago.

Cooking a Pizza

By Todd Braden

Making pizza is easy as long as you do a little bit of planning and follow a few golden rules. The big secrets aren't really secrets but are the things that we all tend to *not* do. Just do your best to not over-do it, use the *best* ingredients you can, and take notes for next time. Unless you are going to start making forty to fifty pizzas a day, every day, you might want to journalize what you did—what worked and what didn't work. Plan what you would do differently next time, and then next time, work your plan.

If your Italian great-grandmother did not leave you her secret recipe for pizza dough that you can make in a small quantity, you may want to look outside for some help. Go to the local pizzeria and ask if you can buy a dough ball. Tell them what size pizza you are making. Their dough is probably fresh and has never been frozen. If not, try the different things that you can find. Take notes. Was it good?

The dough ball from the local shop won't come with directions, so here are a few simple tips. Work it out with a small bit of white flour. Start with a tablespoon on the counter or a cutting board. Pizza can be messy so just accept it. Knead that flour onto the dough ball until it's not sticky and there are no bubbles. Stretch or roll it out as far as you can. Keep it thin. Keep using flour on your surfaces to keep it from sticking to anything. Take notes.

Experiment and try different sauces as "pizza sauce." I prefer the thicker sauces and don't use anything that is too watery. Any part of the pizza that isn't painted with pizza sauce should be painted with olive oil or butter. Don't use too much pizza sauce. You should be able to barely see the dough through it in places, in my opinion.

Add mozzarella. Just enough to cover the pizza sauce and not a bit more. Add cooked or dried meats and sausages. Use quality stuff. Just don't use too much. I prefer a thin pizza because it actually cooks through and doesn't get too soggy.

For your first few pizzas, limit yourself to five toppings. That's including the sauce and the cheese. Sauces don't have to be tomato-based. Olive oil, Alfredo, pesto, refried beans, peanut sauce. Try what you like; just don't use too much! Mozzarella is a great cheese for pizza and I typically shred it. I prefer an even spread of shredded cheese over the sauce, but others prefer chunks. Three toppings left. Choose wisely. Cooked sausage with onion and olives? Artichoke hearts, sun dried tomatoes, and cooked bacon? Cooked chicken, spinach, and garlic? The possibilities are endless. Use what you like.

Take notes and *don't use too much* of anything. You're not making a casserole. You're making a pizza. Have all of your ingredients out and ready. Go quickly. You should let as little time pass between stretching the dough and hitting the oven as possible, because that pizza dough likes to stick to everything and anything, and that flour only keeps it at bay for so long.

The hardest thing to do at home is cook it. This is the part that you have to figure out based on the equipment you have. A preheated hot stone is preferred as long as you can get the pizza to slide onto it. There is an art to this process, and it can be difficult. There are screens out there that allow the bottom to cook as well, but they can be tricky and sticky. I've even heard people use baking mats. Just cook it hot, and cook it fast. Be sure to use a paddle (or peel) to get it in and out of the oven so that you have a sturdy hold of it. Move slowly and purposefully. Let the pizza set for a few minutes. Gaze in awe at what you made. And take notes! Because the best pizza (you've) ever made didn't make itself and probably won't make itself next time either.

CHAPTER VIII

Fancy Stuff

Working hard, educating yourself, being a good patriot, and taking care of your family and those in your community are all important aspects of being a man. But there is much more to it; there's the *fancy stuff*. In this chapter, we hit the bare-bones minimum. Any man, anywhere in the world, should be able to make a cocktail confidently, look good as he's making it, drink it with class, and share it with his friends. Unless, of course, he has a drinking problem; then he should probably not drink it at all or he will wind up hanging out in a pool of his own vomit.

Once you have a couple of cocktails in you, you are looking sharp, you might meet a lady, and then you need to know how to treat her right. We wrap this chapter up with one of the most important aspects of being a man, and that's how to kiss a woman. To be sure, there are many, many more fancy things a guy should know: how to select wine, how to arrange flowers, how to blanch asparagus, and how to build an improvised explosive device to use in an ambush, but, as I said, these are the bare minimum in order to get you moving in the right direction.

Cocktails

Mitch Gerads is an artist that I originally met through another friend of mine, Larry, who contributed the pistol part of this book. Larry got us in touch because I was looking for an illustrator. Mitch and I got together at a bowling alley, kind of a hipster joint in Minneapolis, to talk about the book. I ordered a beer and he ordered an old fashioned.

I like to know people that I'm going to work with, so I asked him a bunch of basic stuff. How he got his start in artistry and whatnot. He showed me some of his incredible work, and it turned out we struck up a friendship almost immediately. At that time, I had already interviewed another artist, but I could not help be completely impressed with Mitch's work. We talked a little while, had some more drinks, ate some food, and then it occurred to me because he's such an impressive dude, I actually asked Mitch, instead of illustrating the book, if he would write a section of the book.

This came about because of the cocktail he was having, the old fashioned. I asked him if he knew how to make that, and he said it was one of his specialties and that, in fact, he knew how to make all of the cocktails I planned on having in the book. Another reason I felt very comfortable asking Mitch to be in the book, instead of illustrating it, was because he told me as he's an up-and-coming artist; he was working as a graphic artist but decided that he wanted to follow his passion and be an illustrator, so that is what he did. He quit his job as a graphic artist, and he applied himself wholeheartedly to what turns out is his life's work. When I said, "Hey, Mitch, I'd like to give a new artist who has never been published a shot," he wholeheartedly agreed that that was the right thing to do. That's why he's so damn impressive.

Anyway, I would encourage you to try these cocktails that Mitch is going to tell you about. You probably don't want to try them all at one time or you'll wake up thinking that a cat pooped in your mouth.

Making Drinks

By Mitch Gerads

Mitch Gerads is currently based out of Phoenix, Arizona. Accomplished in both the commercial art field and the comic book industry, Mitch is the co-creator of the military thriller series, *The Activity*, from Image Comics and the artist on Marvel's *The Punisher*. In case you are unfamiliar with "The Punisher" that is the symbol Chris Kyle and the guys wore on their body armor.

I almost always have a well taken care of, but imposing, beard. You know, to outwardly project how much of a Man I am. It usually works, until someone offers to buy me a beer. You see, I don't drink the stuff, never have, and I'm telling you now, never will. I have tried it, but I just don't like it...at all. However, my manliness stays intact with the always present but growing craft cocktail movement. So instead of beer-hero worshiping Burt Reynolds and Toby Keith, I get to project James Bond and Don Draper. So, if you're like me, Bond, or Draper (or just want to be), here are my thoughts on some classic and very manly cocktails.

Things to consider first:

Stay away from rail or low-shelf spirits because they cost less for a reason. They're full of impurities that lead directly to that hangover the next morning. As a general rule: Stay classy.

Shaken vs. stirred: the process by which the drink is mixed with ice in the shaker or in the serving glass.

Garnish. We're not savages. We're men. The garnish isn't just there for looks; a garnish will bring out a certain flavor used in the drink.

The Classic Martini – 007's second sidearm, next to his PP7. (I don't condone the use of firearms with alcohol—unless you've got a valid LTK permit issued from Her Majesty's Secret Service.) Traditionally…

1oz. dry vermouth and 4 oz. gin or vodka, depending on your preference.

Shaken not stirred. (It's a famous phrase for a reason.) Strain into a martini glass. Garnish with an olive—and olive juice if you like to play and drink "dirty."

Alternatives:

The Sidecar – This is the drink I am most known for, my PP7 of cocktails. It's a tastier, smoother martini but still composed of manly ingredients. Fun fact: The sidecar was one of the most popular drinks during Prohibition.

3 oz. cognac, 1.5 oz. Cointreau, and 1.5 oz. fresh lemon juice. Shaken. Strain into a martini glass. Garnish with an orange peel.

Manhattan – Refined. Classy. Manly.

2 oz. rye or bourbon whiskey, ¾ oz. sweet vermouth, 4 dashes of bitters.

A Manhattan is never shaken, always stirred. I imagine it's what Bond villains must drink. Strain into a martini or cocktail glass. Garnish with a cherry—a brandied cherry if you have them.

There are a million variations on the classic martini. Experiment.

Highball – Technically, not a drink. A "highball" refers to the type of glass the cocktail is served in. Traditionally, a cocktail consisting of a base spirit and a carbonated mixer like tonic, club soda, or pop*, resulting in drinks such as a gin and tonic or a rum and Coke. *I personally don't drink any cocktail mixed with pop/soda. It's not very manly, and the impurities in the sugar will bring back that hangover monster.

Fun Fact: A highball drink served in an old fashioned glass is called a "lowball."

Old Fashioned – Don Draper's drink of choice. There's something about a well-crafted old fashioned that will instantly make you feel like you're the coolest, most suave guy in the room—and, if you're ordering an old fashioned, you probably are.

2 oz. bourbon or rye whiskey, .5 oz. simple syrup (Demerara if you've got it.), and 2-3 dashes of bitters. Lightly stir and serve with a large ice cube. You generally want a single large ice cube to keep your drink cold because it won't melt as fast, watering down your drink. Super unmanly. Impress people by getting an ice sphere mold. Garnish with an orange peel. Sip and feel your chest hair grow.

Alternative:

The Wisconsin version – The old fashioned is a very regional drink. This is my own term for the version that you will find at most bars when out and about. It's still manly, so don't be put off; it's just a less…classy… mix. The bartender will muddle sugar, an orange peel, and a cherry at the bottom of your glass, then pour the spirit over the top, and top off with club soda or water.

There are a million more man-approved cocktails out there. I hope I've given you a few go-to's to keep in your ordering arsenal for when beer isn't cutting it. Next time you go out, and all your buddies order a "brewski," order a bourbon and we'll see who looks like the alpha male. HooRah!

Polishing Shoes

Although SEALs are exposed to polishing boots in, well, boot camp, we master the art in BUD/S, and then promptly forget again following graduation. I can affirmatively say that, overall, SEALs may possibly be the worst-dressed Sailors around. This bothers some SEAL Master Chiefs, one retired West Coaster in particular I can think of, but I have never cared if the guys did not look exactly alike as long as what they were wearing was functional. However, during our time in BUD/S, we have to care about shining our shoes and do it very well. Fortunately, we only had to shine our boots whenever we were going to go stand watch on the quarterdeck or before inspections. The consequence of not shining your shoes to a very high degree for either one of these occasions was what they called "making a sugar cookie." This meant you had to run into the ocean, and then get out in order to roll around in the soft sand until you were covered. However much fun it may sound like, it is not.

For this, I fall back to a friend of mine. I've talked about him before—Rob who sharpened his knife into basically a lightsaber. In fact, he did everything well, including shining his shoes. Rob shined them with cotton balls, which I found rather interesting. I don't know that he needed to do them with cotton balls—he just did. You may be unaware of the fact that shoe polish serves an important function when it comes to footwear. Although shoes used to be made mostly out of leather, now they're made out of many other materials. I like to call them "leather plated." Anyway, shoe polish is made of wax, some oils, and other ingredients that help protect the leather. As the leather is worn down, rubbing polish over the surface of the shoe extends its life.

However, just like so many things, it seems, someone in the military took this perfectly practical, enjoyable, and relaxing activity and turned it into a nightmare. They discovered that if you vigorously rub polish repeatedly with a cloth or other material, it would come to a high shine. And that shine would be even more vibrant if you "spit-shined"—where you actually put some polish onto your boot and then spit on it.

As I said, shoes used to be made of leather mostly, and a lot of them still are, military shoes in particular and fancy pants shoes. You should be shining these things, I believe, because, frankly, even if you're a civilian and you have very expensive shoes, if you don't shine them, you just kind of look like a dick. You're telling people that you can afford these incredibly high-end shoes, and you're not even going to take the time to polish them because you can just buy new ones. If you're in the military, as I said, and you're standing at inspection, you better damn well have them shined like glass.

If you've got a leather boot or shoe in front of you, go ahead and pull it out. Take a good look at this shoe or boot. You'll notice that there are little teeny pits inside that leather, and that's because the leather used to be attached to an animal. Leather is—or was, rather—animal skin. I guess it still is. The key to getting that animal skin shiny is to initially fill those pores with the polish. You're going to start with the rag or a brush, and apply a thick layer of polish onto the boot. After you do this, rub it in and let it sit.

You'll notice that there's a lot of polish on the surface. You want it to be completely dry before you pick up your buffing brush and start hitting it. It's easiest if you stick your hand inside the boot so you can hold it up and turn it as needed. Very simply, after this first application of polish, you're going to take your buffing brush and run it quickly over the boot in all directions until it's at least uniform on the surface and it doesn't have a pale, milky look to it.

After you've done this, pick up your rag or your polish application brush and repeat this process, progressively putting less and less polish on the boot as the pores become full and a uniform coat of polish covers the boot. Once this happens, you can transition to a buffing cloth and a little bit of fluid. This does not ... say it again ... *does not* have to be spit, but you can take any type of vessel, fill it up with water, and dip it into there, meaning the cloth full of polish. This is what Robert used the cotton balls for.

It's going to take some practice, but stick with it. The best part is, even if you scuff this, drop it, or whatever, you'll be able to repeat the process. Or maybe that's the worst part about this because every time I've stood in one of those BUD/S inspections, I wound up scraping the crap out of my boots and just had to redo it again the next week. If you really want to be Johnny Fancy Pants, you can buy something called Military Edge Dressing, a black liquid that comes in a little bottle. You take that and rub it on the soles of your boots. Please don't be a jackass, and understand that I'm just talking about the *edges* of the soles of your boots. I seriously know someone is just going to go out there and paint their shoes, and then slip on them, and then try and raise a ruckus, so use your head.

That is all there is to shining a boot. Good luck, and I hope you don't become a sugar cookie.

Ties

My friend Donnie Rugg is from New York, and he sounds like it. Donnie is not only larger than life but he is also the only haberdasher I've ever met. My wife and I became friends with Donnie and his wife, Sandee, years ago, and we've grown together as friends. Donnie is always very well dressed, and I like to call him the Tailor to the Sailors because he volunteers his time to help military guys get fitted for civilian clothing when they're separating from the service, and then he cuts them pretty good deals. I know this from personal experience.

In New York City, he was involved in the fashion industry in the 1970s and 1980s and had his own line of clothing for a while. Donnie decided that he wanted to become a teacher after the fashion industry, so he went back to college and graduated with his teaching credential on the backside of 50. He is a man of faith and service. He is a patriot. He now teaches young people how to be men and women *not* males and females. For the longest time, I was sure that Donnie moved to California as part of a witness protection program. However, I'm almost positive that that's not true, and if it is, Donnie, I'm sorry; it was great being friends.

Character Makes the Man, Clothes Are Optional

By Donny Rugg

The tie will always make a statement. It is an essential component of your wardrobe and should represent appropriateness with style and individuality. One basic and important function is the presentation at an interview. You should always consider your audience, interviewer, and situation. The function of the tie is to be professional and exude confidence, which, in turn, gains attention and respect for your attire and audience. If you are in a conservative environment, do not be "flashy" with bright colors or patterns.

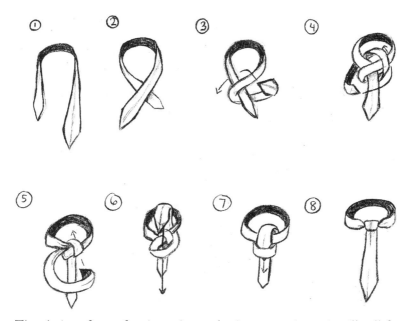

The choice of your first interview or business meeting suit will call for a white shirt as it provides a background for the tie presentation. The tie becomes the focal point. Consider this when selecting the appropriate type: "What suit am I wearing, blue, gray, or perhaps a conservative pin stripe?" Blue should be the first choice. Avoid a red tie on the first interview. Although red exudes power subliminally, it will be more effective on the second interview, which will then exude confidence. Striped ties for an interview are fine; however, once again, avoid bright colors such as oranges, limes, and bright blues. A yellow tie with a small pattern will always show taste and appropriateness. Small patterns are totally acceptable, but it is important to be conscious of size. Never wear flowers or polka dots to an interview, and these are rarely appropriate for a business meeting. The patterns should have color combinations that do not "clash" with the suit. Respect your audience. Note: Bow ties can work, but you must be able to tie one correctly! Same rules apply.

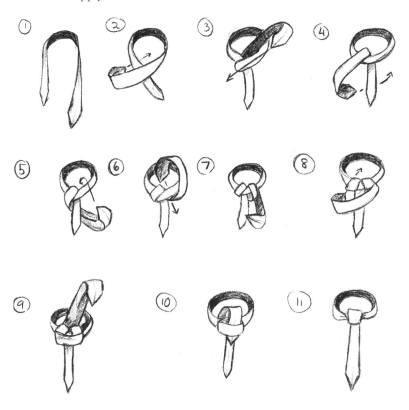

The second interview or business meeting suit choice will be either gray or pinstripe. These are the "uniforms" for interviewing. Blue shirts should be utilized in these situations. Always keep in mind that color combinations with blue should be toned down so as not to show a disorganized combinational thinking. Your choice in ties will always reflect you. Choose wisely for the interviewer or business contact; they will be taking it all in subliminally without a word said. Choosing the correct shirt for your tie is imperative. Striped shirts or tattersall patterns work but must remain in a neat repeat, and the tie must work with the colors in *both* of these patterns. The use of patterns will present a confident statement. Note: Again, bow ties can work but you must be able to tie one correctly!

Everyday tie function should consider the industry, environment, and, again, who you are working with. Know these facts beforehand. The impression you make represents you and the company you represent. "Visuality" has no words but will always have an effect. Wrong decisions on a tie selection can create an impression, perhaps unfairly, of being unsure or unknowing. Men who dress appropriately always notice other men who are appropriately attired. Your tie is the first glance and first chance! Always know your audience, and play to it.

Tying knots is varied, usually individualistic; however, the collar and symmetry are very important. The collar length and spread must be considered. Fashion will dictate the style; whether or not you follow will be important. For example: You do not want a button-down short collar with a Double Windsor Knot. The button-down collar, if desired, should have a longer pointed collar to accommodate that choice in knot. Button under as well. The correct choice would be a spread collar for that knot or an artesian collar, which has longer and wider characteristics. Do not overwork, and both the knot and the thickness of the tie lining must be taken into account. A half Windsor, or once-around knot, shows a style of its own, but remember to secure it tightly under the button and try to have a "valley" centered in the fabric slightly below the knot.

The neck sizing is important as well. A tight neck indicates lack of fit and will be prominent. Too loose looks as if a poor choice was made. Remember the tie and shirt are one! No short collars. If your knot is greater than your collar symmetrically…change it! Do not let your knot drop down below the button; keep it secured by tightening it and raising it up slowly. Your attention to detail in choosing the correct tie and structure will make an impact. Your tie length should be at your belt line…no higher! Be prepared, have style, and always know your audience!

Sew a Button

You may be asking yourself why a Navy SEAL should be qualified to tell you how to sew. The reason is, prior to September 11, 2001 and a drastic increase in the budget, believe it or not, SEALs had to make a lot of their own equipment. In each SEAL Team there is a "para loft," which means a parachuting loft used for packing and repairing parachutes. Inside this space there is also a series of large industrial sewing machines. We used to sit around and try to figure out how to make it easier to carry our equipment. Once we figured something out, we would either manufacture the pouches for rifle magazines, or radios, or medical equipment, or other ideas. Then, we'd figure out how to sew them onto our load-bearing vests or load-bearing equipment in order to be able to carry the maximum amount of equipment with the greatest amount of comfort.

A lot of this went by the wayside with the advent of several different companies that manufacture pre-made equipment. In a way, I'm glad that this happened because you no longer have to spend time in the para loft, but, as an older guy, I'm also a little bit unhappy at the same time. By sewing and working on our own equipment, I think it helped all of us achieve a better understanding of the construction and function. We knew everything inside and out, because, in fact, we had manufactured it from the inside out.

There are many garments that can be repaired by basic sewing, but one in particular that SEALs never need to worry about is underwear. You may have heard the term "going commando," and this is exactly what it means. I have no idea how this saying got started, but, for some reason, it really stuck with SEALs. However, SEALs weren't the original commandos, so I don't know where this phrase came from. I guess it's not important. Anyway, most SEALs don't wear underwear. That's just a fact. For us in particular, since we are in the sand so often, if we wore underwear it would chafe the skin and nether regions.

During one particular training mission, while we were conducting Military Operations in Urban Terrain or (MOUNT) operations, we were in a gunfight at night with the Opposition Force (OPFOR), and it was time for me to run across the street. It was dark, and I was not wearing night vision goggles, so I didn't spot the single strand of barbed wire that had been stretched across the street and ran into it right at crotch level. I figured since I was a hairy-chested freedom fighter, that I should be able to power through it. I made it about ten feet, stretching this thing tight like a rubber band, until finally I couldn't move any longer, and it shot me backward. I skidded on my ass across the street, just like you would see in a cartoon. Although it was embarrassing, what was most disconcerting was that the barbed wire had caught my pants, and ripped the entire front from my belt to about midway down my thigh.

As this was SEAL training and not a little league game, I didn't get to call time out and ask for a new pair of pants. So, I continued to fight all through the night with my friends, and then I extracted the next morning. The entire time, things were a little *breezy*, if you understand what I'm saying. I definitely took some ribbing from the other guys. After I returned home, I gave the pants to my wife who is a fantastic seamstress, and thought nothing more of it.

When it came time for me to return to training, I happened to have the same repaired pants with me. When I put them on, I spotted a colorful patch on the inside—my wife had used some heart-pattern fabric that said, "I love you." Now, granted, I greatly appreciated the sentiment; however, my Chief didn't feel the same way. He really couldn't understand the fact that here was a new Navy SEAL training for combat wearing "I love you" pants.

Why sew a button? Because it can make all of the difference. First, pick the right size button for the buttonhole. Hopefully, if a button falls off, you have one of a similar size to replace it with. If not, get one. Take the thread and a needle, run the thread through the needle, double it up, and then tie several knots into the end. Place the button where you want it, start on the back side of the material, and push it through one of the holes. Now, this is going to be just like changing a tire. You're going to go from one hole to the hole opposite, repeat that several times, then switch over until you're making a cross or diamond pattern, depending on how many buttonholes there are.

Once it gets to the back side, and you're sure that it's secure enough, go ahead and tie the thread off, using, most likely, a Square Knot. How you do that is, you partially run the thread through the material until there's an end—don't let it go all the way through—snip off the needle, and use that material to tie your Square Knot.

Laundry

Doing laundry is not appreciated as a man skill. I do not mean to offend anyone's feminine sensibilities, but it is just a fact. With that said, unless you know how to do laundry or can afford to dry clean everything, you better learn, or you are never going to get a date because you are going to look like a rumpled pile of hobo and live a long, lonely life.

Let me tell you about laundry. On the same trip that I talked about going to Vietnam, after we had been there for a while, we started turning our laundry into the hotels we were staying at to get it washed. After a couple of weeks, I started noticing thin spots in my pants and shirts that I had just bought to go over on this trip. One morning, the group was sitting around having breakfast and I commented, "Man, this seriously looks like they have been doing our laundry by banging them with rocks in a stream," and everyone agreed; our stuff looked wrecked.

A couple of days later, when we came home at our lunchtime and looked at the stream in front of our hotel, there was a bunch of ladies with our shirts and pants, banging them on rocks in a stream. Sometimes things are exactly what they seem. I guess we should have checked beforehand to see if they had washing machines.

I am going to assume that you either own or have access to a washing machine or, at a minimum, a couple of rocks and a stream.

I'm going to let you in on a little-known secret here. Almost every article of clothing has a little tag on it that tells you where it was made and how to wash it. Just grab a shirt and check it out, and, on top of the inside of almost every lid of a washing machine—assuming you don't have one of those front-loading, fancy-pants washers—are directions on how to use the washing machine.

The most important thing about this whole deal is, like everything else we've talked about, preparation. First, gather your dirty clothes. Second, divide them into garments that are mostly white and those that are colored. Generally speaking, when you are washing the whites, you use bleach and detergent, and when you are washing colored clothing, unless you have color-safe bleach, you will only use detergent. Please keep in mind to use only the amount of detergent that is suggested on either the box, jug, or on the washing machine itself. In this case, more is not better. If you are my age, you should remember an episode of *The Brady Bunch* where one of the girls used way too much detergent and it overflowed bubbles. Alice, the housekeeper, got really mad, if I remember correctly.

Next, read the tag on the shirt as well as the directions on the box of the detergent and inside the washing machine lid.

An interesting story: When I was training with a multinational group of folks, one group of the guys was from Canada. After throwing laundry into the washer, you would normally go goof off and come back and then throw it into the dryer after a bit. Once you had it in the dryer, you would go goof off again and then when you come back and you would normally find your clothing it in a big pile of wrinkled crap on top of the washing machine. However, I walked into the laundromat on the base, and my laundry was folded very nicely and separated. I thought it was incredibly strange.

When I returned to where the guys were hanging out, I said, "Hey, did somebody fold my laundry?"

And this guy, Tom, who was from Canada, answered, "Yeah, I folded your laundry."

"Why did you do that?" I asked.

"Well, it would be pretty rude if you pull someone's laundry out of the dryer and just pile it up on the table or something like that. We all fold each other's laundry when we take it out."

I thought that this was very courteous. As a matter of fact, Canadians maybe the most courteous people I've ever met. My son has told me two fun facts about Canada: the first one is that, if you throw a snowball at someone in Canada and hit them, they will actually pick the snow back up, reform it into a ball, and hand it back to you; the second is that, if you are sad in Canada, the government will send someone over to cry for you. You cannot ask for much more than that. The third one is what we just discussed. They will fold your laundry for you. That is just straight nice.

Kissing a Girl

I first met Johnathon Schaech a few years ago at a screening of a movie I had a part in, *Act of Valor*, in Hollywood. After the screening, Johnathon came up and started telling me I was a good actor, and he was excited about my performance. I immediately thought that either, one, he was a liar, or, two, he didn't know anything about acting. When I went home and looked up Johnathon's credits, I found out that neither one was true. He's not a liar, and he certainly knows a hell of a lot about acting.

Johnathon has gone out of his way to help me. By this, I mean that he has really taken the time to explain to me the finer points of acting and what it's like to be a part of the entertainment industry. He also vouched for me with director Michael Risley and got me a role in a short film called *"Azadah"*. It means "Hope" in Pashto. In a strange twist of fate, I play a USMC Colonel and John plays an Special Forces guy. So, in other words, Michael took him at his word and risked destroying his project by having me in it playing opposite Johnathon. I will always be grateful to Johnathon for that. I also think it should be noted that Johnathon is 5 days older than me, but still looks like he's twenty-two. I'm not sure I appreciate that.

Kissing a Girl

By Johnathon Schaech

I'm an actor in a lot of movies—some good, some bad, some famous, some not so famous. My highlights have been opposite Jon Voight, Tom Hanks, and the author of this book. (Oh and Ed Harris, Jessica Lange, etc.) But, most importantly, I'm the father of Camden and the husband of Jules. Follow me on twitter @johnschaech.

How to kiss a girl?

First off, a man needs to respect a woman before he can truly kiss her. Much like Derrick, I am the kind of man who opens doors for women and buys my wife flowers when the feeling strikes me.

I have learned the art of kissing a woman both professionally and personally. I'm a professional actor and have kissed some very famous lips, but nothing has felt better than kissing my wife's gorgeous lips over and over again. It's a skill every man must have in order to obtain the woman of his dreams.

Now, one must know that the lips are the most sensitive part of the body. They are a tactile sensory organ and can be very erogenous. A kiss is usually the start of either a great love affair or the greatest betrayal a human heart can give, but the act of kissing can be defined and taught.

The basic mechanics of kissing seem simple, but to really kiss a girl in a way that will make her want to see you again and again is an art form. Before attempting the kiss, one must look for the signs that a kiss will be accepted. Girls will generally give signs such as conscious or unconscious touching. If she looks in your eyes longer than normal, if she compliments your eyes, your face, and especially your lips, she wants you to kiss her.

So take the lead and kiss her. Start slowly. Start steadily, and remain calm and confident. (Nothing is worse than being overly aggressive or using your tongue when you go in for a first kiss.) It's simple. She wants your lips to touch hers. Allow the senses to be awakened both on your lips and on hers.

Use your hands appropriately. Yes, gentlemen, put your hand—gently—in her hair when you go in for a soft kiss. This added sensation will let her know you want her. Women long to be the one and also to find the one…so be the one. This added touch can make your life and the kiss much more effective.

However, if she has on a wig like Gwyneth Paltrow did in the movie *Hush*, you may want to stay away from that area and go for the small of the back or rub your fingers softly on the back of the neck. Both are very arousing areas.

Now, gents. Make sure to check your breath. Altoids are the favorite when on the set, and a good brushing is what makes my wife most pleased. You can have Warren Beatty's looks and lips, but if you have bad breath, you are not going to get the results you so desperately desire.

Relax, and remember it's a girl you're kissing—so go in soft and gentle, but with enough confidence to really push your sensory pads onto hers in order to get a—*response*. That's the key to your success.

The art of kissing a girl is that every girl is different, and you need to quickly figure out what she likes. Be open to the response she gives, and go from there. You may place both your upper and lower lips on her top lip, then go down to the lower lip. You might feel her lips parting—this is her telling you she wants more of the same. You may find her eyes open or closed—it's best to close yours slightly as your lips meet. (And it goes without saying you slightly cock your head, right? Every man knows to slightly cock his head when kissing a girl or you'll bump noses.)

After the act, always be complimentary and grateful for the opportunity to place your lips on hers. Trust me—with that as your mantra, you can't go wrong.

CHAPTER IX
Campfire Stories

I have mentioned repeatedly throughout this book that men learn from other men. The passing of knowledge through stories and oral tradition is as old as spoken language. It is as old as man's ability to make fire. Prior to the written word, this is how histories were relayed from generation to generation. Men used to gather around a campfire and tell stories. This activity is still a significant and substantial way for many cultures to bond. In this respect, nothing has really changed in my world, meaning the world of the SEAL Teams. Whenever there is a chance to start a fire and hang out around it, SEALs will do so. This is a perfect venue to tell stories and share common experiences, pass on the legends of bravery, what to do and what not, lessons learned, and simply have a good time.

As I'm trying to possibly make a small change in the way our culture looks at manhood, I cannot think of a better thing to do than actually share with you some "campfire stories" as it were. The men that I've asked for these stories have all proven themselves in the world one way or another, but, more importantly, they're all truly men. They've had the opportunity to do good and bad, and they have collectively chosen to do good. Just like the other parts in the book where my friends have explained how to do tasks, these are their words. Each of these stories tells a bit about them and is a glimpse inside of their soul. At their root, each also reflects a key lesson that we, as men, should take with us every day.

Hank Paul

Honorary Chairman of the Board SP Productions

Hank is my friend's father, and I met him by chance inside his office building one day. He is over eighty years old now, and is a classy gentleman. Each morning, Hank makes it a practice of hanging a new quote on the corkboard inside the elevator so you can read it as you're traveling up and down to different offices. These aren't simply happy little quotes. They're actually often very insightful and deeply meaningful. To me, this practice symbolizes Hank in that he is constantly moving, looking for new things to share with other people, and instilling knowledge and wisdom. We had the chance to talk for a while, and he conveyed the following story to me. I was struck by something remarkable Hank touched on: the fact that as a young, newly married man would answer his nation's call without question and go on to have some *very* strange experiences. It seems like men are no longer cut from the cloth that Hank Paul is, and I wanted him to have a chance to share some of his memories with you.

By Hank Paul

In Judaism, our bar mitzvah meant something special to a thirteen year old: "You are now a man and are now responsible for all of your actions." The word "responsibility" resonated with me, even at an early age. Whether it be with my family, my children, or my friends, and setting an example. Everything. So that is where part of that foundation came.

When WWII broke out, we had most roughly five generations of fellows on the street because there was one block about the size of a football field that had maybe three thousand people of all different generations. The older guys that got drafted were like brothers to us. They took care of us, listened to us, and we looked up to them. Of those fellas, four from the neighborhood got killed, one who had lived right next door to me and the rest on the street. It was quite interesting because that was my first time experiencing that type of anguish and pain. When a telegram came, the mother of one of them screamed. I could see that. And you saw the gold star in the windows of a number of them. I was really affected by it.

In 1952, the Korean War was on. I knew that it was just a matter of time. I left for Fort Leonard Wood, Missouri for basic training and engineering training. There was a talk on the atomic bomb and so on, and then, when it came time, we got a notice to go to Nevada. We traveled on the train, and, when we got there, they didn't tell us much and handed each of us a gas mask. They got us down into a trench that was perhaps ten feet tall and insisted that, if we were below ground, we would be safe and wouldn't have to worry about radiation. The interesting thing was, the people who were telling us this were on loud speakers, way back in some closed building. We didn't know anything because we didn't know what to expect.

And then they began to count down to zero. And since light travels faster than sound, they had us turn our backs and close our eyes. The light was so strong that I could see it through closed lids. The sound was so loud I thought my chest was going to fall apart. Then, I don't know exactly how much time passed in between, they had us march into the radiation. It was hot and misty and we saw animals dead on the ground, some blind because they were out there. I guess they were doing some kind of experiment, and we walked forward, and then at some particular point they had us come back, take off our clothes, masks and everything, get showers, and get dressed. We went back to wherever we were staying, and then we left on a train.

Not long after the trip, we began to hear about the radiation and so on. People were worried. I made up my mind and said, "This is just another experience, whatever it is." I was asked to serve. I didn't know exactly what this would mean, but I wasn't going against the government, and I wasn't going to get involved in anything.

It was my responsibility in serving.

It seemed everything my generation did growing up was very cohesive and patriotic. We collected scrap metal, and we had a contest against other streets and, "We had more," or "You had more," but, of course, Uncle Sam always won. But that was part of it.

Today, you see they are trying not to have scores and so on. No competition. Again, it is another thing that they are killing in people. From sports, we learned about life. I played one year of high school football. I had a great coach, but the biggest thing I learned, which I used in my sales career throughout my life, was "Don't lay on that ground, get up."

One day at practice, I had been knocked down in a scrimmage. When I took a long time getting up, the coach came running over with that bamboo stick and whacked it across my rear end.

"Up!" he yelled. "You don't lay there!"

He explained that even though the play had continued onto the other side of the field, if I got up to my feet, I may have another chance to make a play because it could come back my way.

You don't lie there. You get up.

This was very important for me. Another concept that stuck with me over the years was the willingness to fail in order to succeed.

I often think about the story of a fellow by the name of Pasin, who was an immigrant from Italy that came to America as a cabinetmaker. He carried his tools in a little wagon that he built. Still, everywhere he went, he said he couldn't get a cabinet job. They all wanted him to make this wagon. As it turned out, that wagon was the Radio Flyer little red wagon, and eventually he had built a major company. And his son, of course, worked with him, and, when Pasin retired, he said, "Son, I'd like you to do something for me. Make as many mistakes as you can." He said, "Because that's how you learn, and they are opportunities, so don't worry about a mistake because what a mistake is and you look at it...It just means that it is another way to do it, perhaps another way. It's not a tattoo, it's not something that's wrong."

I was fortunate enough to grow up during World War II and the Korean War. This may sound strange now, but it helped me appreciate the things I have. I love my children and grandchildren. To hear them say, "If I can follow in your footsteps, grandpa, I'd be happy." If you hear that you say, "Well, maybe I didn't do anything special but I've got to set an example of who I am." If you do that, they learn by watching you, not by what you tell them, but only by what you do.

My Thoughts:

Hank left his young wife, Dorothy, to head off to war. Not because he wanted to, but because it was his duty as an American. He did not know if he would see her again. He walked into a nuclear blast for his country. What is remarkable is that after his service, he hung up his uniform and returned to civilian life. He did not complain or demand an apology from the government. He simply returned to life and prospered. That is a man.

Scott Waugh

Founder of Bandito Brothers

I met Scott Waugh along with Mouse McCoy and Jacob Rosenberg when I was filming the movie *Act of Valor*. If you haven't seen it yet, it is truly a piece of American cinematic genius. That was the movie that was made in order to really increase the recruiting into the SEAL Teams so that we could continue to have future generations. It is a solid action movie that tells the stories of Frogmen. Scott, Mouse, and Jacob Rosenberg are the owners of the studio. They cooked up the idea along with some guys at Naval Special Warfare Command, particularly a guy named Duncan Smith.

The truth be told, if it were not for these guys, you would not be reading this book right now, because they made the decision to out me as a SEAL in that movie and that led to this. I have taken a bunch of crap for being "Hollywood," but I think the positive far outweighs the negative when it comes to this. I think all of these guys are simply grand.

Scotty is a very interesting guy who grew up in Hollywood and around the movie industry. His father, Fred, was a legendary stuntman who was the *original* double for the *original* Spiderman, for real. He had a reputation as a very great guy to work with and be around both because of his professionalism and his personality. Growing up, Scotty had the opportunity to go one of two ways: He could have acted like the child of privilege that he was, taking things for granted, and growing into a punk, or decide to take the other road. That road was to strive to earn the respect of the people around him like his father did. This path entailed working hard, treating people properly, and becoming the best he could be by applying himself on a daily basis. I think Scott has achieved that goal: He's respected as a father, as a husband, as a director, and as a stunt man. I'm proud to call him my friend.

By Scott Waugh

A wise man told me we all start someplace. Most don't join the journey at the finish line. Only a select few who were born on that line feel entitled, but they will always feel lost because they missed the adventure and have no true appreciation. And those of us who have been on a long journey know the goal is a brief moment that disappears in the blink of a second, and the next chapter begins. And we wake up wishing we would have enjoyed the arduous quest it took to get where we currently are. All the people that have influenced us, pushed us, carried us, and privately supported us to live our dreams deserve to be treated with admiration, no matter how insignificant we might think they are. Every man deserves to be treated the same because we are all on our individual paths which will ultimately end abruptly. And we want to leave behind a better place for those that we have loved, that we have touched, everyone who has somehow helped us live our life, whether it's the janitor or the billionaire that funded our dream. We are a grain of sand on an infinite beach. We have a tendency to think that our lives are more important than the rest, but, in the end, we will all end up at the same place. That last heartbeat. That last breath. Then life's journey is complete. Treat others as you would like them to treat you. Oh, and that wise man was my best friend, my confidant, my father.

My Thoughts

The rampant abuse of power, or rather the prevention of this, is one of the reasons I stayed in the Navy. I despise this natural tendency in humans, myself included. To have an example of someone who has had the ability to run wild and treat people without dignity and chooses not to is more than remarkable. It is a choice for all of us.

David Bell

Owner and CEO of School Supplies Delivered

SchoolSuppliesDelivered.com

David Bell is the older brother of one of my best friends from my youth, Joe Bell. Joe, another great friend Eric, and I were the Three Horsemen of the Apocalypse for quite a while. We could not find anyone dumb enough to be the fourth horseman with us. Dave was always a little bit more measured than we were so he was definitely out of the running. He was a high school and college wrestler; it was fascinating watching him wrestle because he always looked so fluid, like he was exerting no effort at all.

Dave was incredibly disciplined, and he constantly worked very hard to be the best. I asked Dave to write a section in this book about taking a calculated risk because, at a certain point in his life, he was doing very well in a former vocation and then decided to start a different business for himself. He gathered all the pertinent facts, made a decision, and, what's more important, he acted on it.

There's another reason I wanted Dave to be in this book. It's because we view the world through different lenses. I'm speaking in particular about our political views. Dave loves his country as much as I do; he just thinks it should be run differently. It is absolutely imperative that we, as men, continue to respect each other even if we have different political views. We are all Americans.

Taking a Risk vs. Gambling

By David Bell

For me, there is a world of difference between taking a risk and gambling. Gambling, to me, is simply playing the odds. It's throwing the dice and leaving the outcome to fate or something completely out of one's control. Taking a risk, on the other hand, is betting on yourself, on your ability to adapt and succeed despite challenges, both known and unknown.

From my experience, people who decide to take that leap do so when the fear of failure becomes manageable. Some do it when they are twenty, and some do it when they are sixty-five, but they all do it when the scary part of betting on oneself is no longer immobilizing. For me, I suppose I learned it in the sport of wrestling in high school and college. To grow in that sport, one gets into situations where risks have to be taken in order to win. One has to be prepared to try different strategies all the time, strategies that may not necessarily be "game ready." Wrestlers learn early not to let the "perfect" be the enemy of the "good." Many times it's their only option to avoid a loss. In wrestling, improving is a direct result of risking defeat to gain an upper hand—and comes to those wrestlers who embrace that risk as part of a process.

A lot of people talk about perseverance through defeat as being essential, and, while there is a lot of truth in that, for me, that's just the beginning. There are invaluable lessons to be learned in defeat. It's more about understanding how one must adapt, and translating that knowledge to action, than it is about taking a fat lip once in a while and not bitching about it.

The contrast of taking a risk and gambling can be widened when one commits to working their ass off in order to turn their goal into a reality. Wanting something and deciding to go get something is a matter of plain hard work. Trying to do a good job is not enough to produce, just as showing up to wrestling practice is not enough win consistently. True commitment to taking the gamble out of risk means that there is intensity and a relentless nature to the approach. I'm reminded of the cartoon depicting a stork with a frog hanging from his beak—and the frog's arms in a chokehold on the stork's neck.

Yet, even more gamble can be taken from risk with resilience. The truth is, in anything, everyone gets fat lips. Sometimes it is hard to remain undeterred and focused. True excellence is not an end result. It is an attitude that, whatever the obstacles, there can be progress. With optimism, self-confidence, and a healthy dose of creativity, no obstacle lasts forever, and great things await those who know the difference between taking a risk and rolling the dice.

My Thoughts

It is possible to be a tough guy and simultaneously care deeply about your fellow man; although these may seem to be, they are not mutually exclusive. It is also possible, and I think imperative, to learn from not winning. You never have to like it, but if you do not use loss as an opportunity, then it is a *real* loss.

Matt Heidt

Matt and I have known each other the entire time that we've been SEALs; this is because we graduated from BUD/S together. Matt is a former Marine, a mortarman— meaning he actually shot mortars—who then decided to join the Navy. Matt being Matt, got out of the Marine Corps in a very interesting manner, by slipping some paperwork for his discharge from the Marine Corps Reserve into his company commander's pile of papers to sign, and he signed them. This shows what I like to call "remarkable initiative." Matt was injured in his original BUD/S class, which was 182, and rolled into my class, which was 184. It was a shock for Matt, I think, because his class was completely squared away and had a relatively easy time compared to ours as far as that goes in the first phase of BUD/S.

I recall Matt being a bit put out by our disorganization and subsequent thrashings after we had been hammered all day, which means doing extracurricular exercise, getting yelled out, spending time in the surf zone, and just getting beaten down by the instructor staff. Matt asked what was wrong with us. We had no frame of reference to understand that BUD/S actually did not have to be as hard as it was for us because we were truly collectively stupid as a class. Who knew?

I honestly had never heard the saying "if you're going to be stupid you better be hard" until after that. It may have been written about us. Matt and his wife, Kristin, remain Sara's and my great friends today.

Legacy

By Matt Heidt

What does it all mean, and to what purpose should a man be striving? At a practical level, each of us has our own path to walk using our talents and passions, hopefully to the best of our ability. But how can we focus our efforts into fruitful and meaningful action? We begin by keeping the end in mind.

Deep within the heart of all men is the desire to make a lasting contribution to our families, our communities, and, ultimately, our world. By considering early in our lives what kind of legacy we wish to leave, we are empowered to hold ourselves accountable for that vision and to become the very best version of ourselves.

I came to the SEAL Teams from the Marine Corps, so when I decided to take that risk of going to BUD/S, I hedged my bet. I joined the Navy as a Hospital Corpsman because I figured that, if for some reason, I didn't complete BUD/S, that I could rejoin the Marines as a corpsman. As it turned out, this decision was more momentous than I realized. Some SEAL Corpsmen (now called Medics) see this additional duty as a burden that confuses their role as a SEAL first or prevents them from participating in training while they act as a safety observer at times. I found that when I was practicing medicine, especially while deployed to developing countries, I became the best version of Matt, as a person. I saved the life of a comrade wounded in a training accident, treated fatal strains of malaria in Kenyan children, and cared for flood victims deep in the jungles of Bolivia. I learned through these experiences that when I was helping others, the very best version of me came to the fore. This realization was the catalyst for understanding not only what it took for me to become contented as a person, but also to recognize the importance of leaving a positive legacy in my wake.

How will your children remember you when you are gone? Keeping this question in your mind is a very powerful source of inspiration and provides a framework for decision-making in your life. Mistakes will be made, to be sure, but acting today with your legacy in mind propels a man forward with purpose. As a real estate investor, it would be a simple matter of buying an office building, putting my name on it, and enjoying a lasting and tangible legacy. But is that really the answer? Tangible though it may be, the Heidt Tower imparts no enduring benefit aside from the financial. Instilling in my children the characteristics of loyalty, honor, humility, integrity, and the value of helping others imbues them with the tools to enjoy a meaningful life. This gift, this legacy, can withstand any hardship or trial, and will not deteriorate, but will grow over time. It is often said that we should live for ourselves, but our life is just a succession of passing moments. Living as an example to those we love provides joy to us in those moments and an inheritance that echoes through eternity.

My Thoughts

One of the greatest things an old man can give a young man is the gift of perspective. Just like anything, though, a gift that is offered is not always accepted. If the younger man accepts this gift, he is starting on the road to wisdom.

Jon Voight

If you have seen a movie or a television show in America in the last forty or so years, then you know who Jon Voight is. Although most know him as the Academy-Award-winning actor, I am fortunate enough to know Jon as a friend. I was first introduced to him prior to deploying to Afghanistan when I was stationed at SEAL Team SEVEN. He came down with Gary Sinise and some of the people from the Medal of Honor Society, including Big Mike Thornton, one of our living SEAL Medal of Honor recipients. They hosted a party for the entire SEAL Team SEVEN at the Crown Room at the Hotel del Coronado. That evening, Jon got up and said some very kind words about the military, I was just a face in the crowd. We met a couple more times after the party throughout the years, and I started to get a better appreciation for Jon. Then we started talking, really as friends, and he conveyed to me some stories, one in particular that struck me. It really revolves around the maturation process of a man and what that really means. What it comes down to is action, not talking. Words are cheap. Saying something and doing something are different. Patriotism isn't about complaining. Patriotism is about acting to do what is right. As we are human, this may not always be done at the perfect time, but it is always the right time to do the right thing.

By Jon Voight

As the war in Southeast Asia, the Vietnam War, raged in the '60s, I had to make a decision about what was going on with the draft. At some point, I decided I wanted to be an actor, and, once I'd made this decision, I didn't want any interruptions. As a result, I decided to enter into the reserves. After completing basic training, I then committed myself to several years, every month, on the weekends, and also a couple of weeks during the summers.

The purpose of all the training was to ensure that you were prepared for battle if you were called upon to go to Vietnam. It was a frightening time because I didn't want to have to go fight in the war. As I said, I was intent on pursuing my choice of profession and excited to continue toward my path to acting. I was like a lot of the other kids and, during my brief time in the service, just didn't want anything to do with Vietnam. Since I was kind of a character, I was trying to have some fun while I was in the service. During boot camp, there were some fellows who were trying to make things difficult for me, which is really what it is all about.

I wasn't all that interested in following orders and doing what I was told. I was a guy who, if somebody told me to do something, I'd say, "Why are you telling me that?" I'd raise a question about it. Well, in the service, you have to follow orders, but it was something I constantly struggled with. While I noticed that there were guys who had been through some stuff and I respected, there were also others in leadership positions that I didn't respect and would never be able to follow.

By the time I had some success in the late '60s in the field of acting, I fell in with people who were very far to the left who were trying to end the war. These groups were the new movement in Hollywood, young kids. Not unlike the young, arrogant kids all over the country at that time who were marching against the war. I got into this toward the end of the '60s, after my time in the service was finished.

Hollywood thought they were smarter than the rest of the country, and they were being brave for being out there. Well, the real bravery was happening in Vietnam with the guys who were trying to liberate South Vietnam and were fighting against the communist forces from the North. But it was a confusing time.

Later on, I saw the Left was saying that the United States was the problem in Vietnam, and, if we pulled out, the two sides, the North and South, would come and embrace and everything would be happiness and joy and love. Well, of course, when we finally pulled out of Vietnam, it was a disaster. The North came in—contrary to what we had promised the South— we didn't defend, we didn't even give them the bullets to defend themselves, and they were overrun. It was a great massacre, a horrific loss of life in Laos, Cambodia, and Vietnam.

When I saw the Left just walked away as if they had nothing to do with it, it made a lasting impact on me. They were the ones that brought the end of the war, the people that were marching, these are people who were friends of mine, who were recommending that everything was going to be just fine. And then somewhere around 2.5 million people were killed in these countries because we had pulled out. That really struck me. I was very disturbed about that moment, and I have this insight because I was part of that movement.

I was aware, finally, we hadn't lived up to our promises to the people in the south of Vietnam. I was aware of the slaughter that took place when we pulled out, all the bloodshed. When I finally saw it myself, I said, "Well, I made mistakes. I mean, there's blood on my hands." There's blood on my hands and the people of my generation who were wooed into thinking other ways about what was going on. We could have liberated that country. It didn't have to fall to communism. It was a long time before I was able to be clear about that, but I was able to get there.

Once I did, I became very saddened by my participation in these events. I wanted to make amends. But then again, as I say, there's this idea of a vocation and the heroic vocations. When we are little kids, it's natural for a young boy to want to be hero. We have the Avengers coming out and all these superheroes from the Marvel Comics and stuff like that. It's feeding something that's unnecessary for the young. They grow up wanting to be heroes.

I think, in my generation, what happened was when Vietnam happened, everybody was saying there are *no* heroes. People were presenting the idea that this portrait of a hero didn't exist, that it was a fiction. They found every way to diminish people who were on the battlefield. We weren't allowed to have those heroes once we hit nineteen or twenty years old in my generation.

As I got older, I realized this was a lie.

There were real heroes. The commitment to defend and serve our great country is a heroic commitment. It's a commitment to sacrifice and to stand in front in harm's way for other people. My dad use used to quote Rudyard Kipling from his poem *Gunga Din* and say, "He's a better man than I am, Gunga Din."

What it meant was that this young fellow of another culture and another race was fighting patriotically for the appropriate cause, and he was doing so in the highest fashion, willingly, with humility, doing everything he could, following orders into hell for this proper cause and idea. But he didn't have to do it.

I had a pretty high estimation of myself during my life. Sometimes it was a false estimation. I thought I was pretty hot stuff for a while there. We came to a part of our country's history where movie stars were heroes. Movie stars are certainly *not* heroes. There's nothing wrong with being a movie actor and doing that job as well as any job. Storytellers are necessary, yes, but they are not heroes. Every day, if you want to see a hero, all you have to do is get down to an army base and take a look at those people who took the oath.

Although I always respected the guys who went to fight in Vietnam, I knew they had no choice and had to go. But, as the years went on, I came to realize that the soldiers who were there following orders and trying to liberate this country were upholding the great legacy of the United States military. I also became more and more aware that, even if these guys did not perform heroically in a certain way, this was a heroic profession, and there was something very extraordinary about these people.

At the same time, I realized my commitment to what I thought was to be life, my profession, was of a lesser vocation. I understood these guys had something extra, just like those people I see in other heroic professions, like my friendship with the first responders on 9/11. We see people who are born to this type of service, and I have the greatest regard for these guys.

As I developed this understanding over the years, I started to align myself with the people who were meeting the planes coming back from the Gulf War, trying to celebrate in whatever way we could the fellows who had fought and were still alive. We also gave our time to those who had fought in Vietnam and never been given a proper welcome home. In 1987, I got involved with a concert for HBO that was called *Welcome Home* and spent a year of my life organizing it. It took place on the Fourth of July in Washington, DC, and it was a wonderful tribute to the Vietnam vets.

Since that time, I've been dedicated more and more to serving the military. I will go to these places, these different celebrations, and just let them know that there are people who understand the greatness of their contribution to our country, their meaning and their true magnificence. They are responsible for the freedom we have that we enjoy in this country. I go to those in our armed forces and thank them from the bottom of my heart. I'm very happy to be among the people who understand their greatness and people like my fellow actor, Gary Sinise, who do everything they can for the military. We all know each other, and we are all very happy being in company with each other.

Today, there has been a revival in real patriotism and genuine support for the troops. There's nobody that won't express a love for the troops in any camp in the United States, regardless of how far left or right or whatever. It's become a standard now that we support our troops, and we admire our troops, and we want to do everything for them. You see, the movie actors now are in the right thinking. They take out time on these PSAs to recommend people; they're going to do everything they can for the wounded warriors and the different foundations that have been set up for the troops. That's very, very admirable. I say it's wonderful. It's a very good use of their persuasive talents.

My Thoughts

Older men have both the advantage and disadvantage of time. With it, we have the ability to reflect on our actions, dissect them, and then either try to repeat the successes accomplished or rectify the wrongs we have done to our fellow man and ourselves. The disadvantage of time is that it is a cruel master, limiting our corrective actions with the chains of this mortal coil. Young men have the advantage of time in that they have the ability to live a life that is fulfilling and fruitful, if they practice wisdom. The disadvantage of youth is that without "time on earth," they simply will never have wisdom as wisdom takes time. Herein lies the necessity of the relationship between old and young. The fulfillment of life for a real man is not the accumulation of earthly goods, or even good deeds. Our fulfillment comes through knowing that we have passed our knowledge to the younger generations, making them worthy of the world that we built for them.

In a final return to the former President Kennedy, one of his better quotes is:

"I can imagine no more rewarding a career. And any man who may be asked in this century what he did to make his life worthwhile, I think can respond with a good deal of pride and satisfaction: 'I served in the United States Navy.'" Although, as a former Sailor, I take pride in this statement, I think Kennedy got it wrong. The most rewarding life choice any male can have is to become a man.

Wrap Up

At best, hopefully, this was a marginally helpful book for you. The worst case is you're going to be pissed at me for the rest of your life and want this time back on your deathbed, just like me with all the legal smack. There's so much more to being a man than can be explained in a single volume, but there's one thing that I can tell you with certainty: That unless you start the journey, you are never going to get there.

And this then begs the question, where is "there"?

To me, "there" is where you want to be. If you're somewhere and you're not happy, you need to take it upon yourself to get up and move. This is not intended to be a shallow statement telling you to run from one pleasure to the next, avoiding responsibility. Do not use this as an excuse to abandon people and obligation. There's a tremendous difference between being unhappy and being inconvenienced. Anything worth having is worth working at. Don't forget this. If you've made a commitment, you need to follow through with it.

So what are the takeaways from this book?

Well, a couple practical skills, but, more importantly, I hope that I've done a sufficient job explaining to you my basic philosophy of manhood. Identifying problems, not just griping about them, but actually applying yourself to figuring out the solution and then doing it. Taking responsibility, serving your fellow man, and judging and treating them according to the content of their character alone. Being strong when others are weak around you, not being afraid to take a stand, and, I think very importantly, doing what is right because it is right, not because you have to.

ACKNOWLEDGEMENTS

If you knew me growing up and followed me through my life and career, there is no way I can possibly describe what has taken place other than Divine Intervention. Thank you, God, for everything. No man is an island, and that could not be truer for me.

On the earthly side, I would like to start by thanking the men and women of Naval Special Warfare. Being a civilian now, it is with great pride that I look at their performance as hyper-patriots. They continue to "Stand the Watch" so that I can goof around with my children and grandchildren. In particular, I need to thank my Chiefs. They are what make the SEAL teams, The Teams. I have also had the opportunity to work with and for some fine SEAL officers who gave me the chance to do my job to the best of my ability. I did not always reach this mark.

My mom worked very hard supporting us as a single mother. To be sure, I was not an easy child to rear, so thanks, Ma. Adam Mitchell, The Mechanic. Well done, wow.

I really want to thank Steven Paul and his crew. Steven had the initiative and vision to see this book was created in what can only be described as a SEAL-like manner. He is also a father and a husband who loves his family and respects them, as a man should.